An American Speaks
アメリカ人が語る

沈む超大国

アメリカの未来
No Future for America

マックス・フォン・シュラー
MAX・VON・SCHULER

ハート出版

アメリカ人が語る
沈む超大国・アメリカの未来

An American Speaks

No Future for America

Introduction
はじめに

Americans like to compare themselves to ancient Rome. In fact, they like to say that they are the heirs to the Roman Empire. Just look at the architecture of the Chicago Museum of Science and Industry, or the New York City Metropolitan Museum of art. It is classical Roman. Perhaps Rome could be called the first "world" Empire. A businessman could travel from what is now Syria, to what is now Britain, and travel in safety, under the same laws and rule of the Roman Empire.

アメリカ人は自分たちを古代ローマと比較したがります。実際、自分たちはローマ帝国の後継者だと主張したがります。シカゴ科学産業博物館やニューヨークのメトロポリタン美術館の建築を見ればわかります。古典的なローマ様式です。ローマは最初の〝世界〟帝国と呼べるかもしれません。当時のビジネスマンは、現在のシリアからイギリスまで、ローマ帝国と同じ法律と支配のもとで、安全に旅をすることができました。

Yet in Rome, the power and glory of ancient Rome gradually declined. So too is America in decline. There are many in Japan who believe America to be something eternal. Yet ancient Rome fell, and crumbled into dust.

しかし、古代ローマの権力と栄光は徐々に衰退していきました。アメリカも衰退の一途をたどっています。日本にはアメリカが永遠の存在であると信じている人がたくさんいます。しかし、古代ローマは没落し、滅びました。

Introduction

In the year 476, King Odoacer of the Germans deposed the last Roman Emperor in the West, Romulus Augustulus. At that time the population of the city of Rome was 1 million people. But after the abolishment of the Roman Empire, the bureaucracy that oversaw the feeding of so many people was also disbanded. After 100 years, the population of the city of Rome fell to some 55,000 people. They were ghosts, living in the ruins of the past.

476年、ゲルマン人のオドアケルが西ローマ帝国最後の皇帝ロムルス・アウグストゥルスを廃位させました。当時のローマ市の人口は100万人。しかし、ローマ帝国の滅亡とともに、これほど多くの人々を養っていた官僚機構も解体されました。100年後、ローマ市の人口は5万5000人ほどにまで減少しました。彼らは過去の廃墟

Chicago Museum of Science and Industry
シカゴ科学産業博物館

The Metropolitan Museum of Art
メトロポリタン美術館

はじめに

に住む亡霊のような存在でした。

It will be difficult for many Japanese people to believe, but present day America will soon suffer the same fate.

多くの日本人には信じがたいでしょうが、現在のアメリカもやがて同じ運命をたどることになります。

I have lived in Japan for 50 years. I have found Japan to be a wondrous land. Yet I have always been amazed by the Japanese attitude towards America. People think America is sort of a shining land of Gods, a world of perfect happiness.

私は日本に住んで50年になります。日本は素晴らしい国だと思います。しかし、アメリカに対する日本人の態度にはいつも驚かされます。アメリカは輝かしい国、世界一幸福な世界であるかのように思われています。

Having been born in America, I know that this is certainly not true. In particular when I first arrived in Japan in 1974, it was the dream of many people to live in America. That is no longer true. In fact, America is facing a great crisis.

アメリカで生まれた私は、それが真実ではないことを知っています。特に私が初めて日本に来た1974年当時は、アメリカで暮らすことが多くの日本人の夢でした。しかし、その理想の世界はもはや真実ではありません。実際、アメリカは大きな危機に直面しています。

Introduction

The truth is, America is moving towards Civil War. I think civil conflict in America is inevitable. In this book I will describe what I see to be the future of life on the North American continent. It will be brutal, and most Americans will not survive. America will cease to exist as a unified nation.

現実には、アメリカは内戦に向かっています。私は、アメリカでの内戦勃発は避けられないと考えています。本書では、私が予測する北米大陸の未来について述べます。それは残酷なもので、ほとんどのアメリカ人は生き残れないでしょう。統一国家としてのアメリカは存在しなくなるでしょう。

What is about to happen, indeed is already happening to America, is not because of devilish intervention by Russia or China. It is totally the work of Americans themselves, for selfish reasons.

これから起ころうとしていること、いや、すでにアメリカで起こっていることは、ロシアや中国の策略によるものではありません。それは完全に、アメリカ人自身の利己的な動機によって引き起こされているのです。

The North American continent has great mineral wealth, a very temperate climate, suited for agriculture, and access to the major oceans of the world for trade. Yet Americans have wasted all this, for selfish and petty reasons.

北米大陸には豊富な鉱物資源があり、温暖な気候は農業に適して

おり、世界の主要な海洋にアクセスでき貿易にも適しています。しかし、アメリカ人は利己的で短絡的な理由で、これらすべてを無駄にしてきました。

The America that emerges from this collapse will be a minor nation, I suspect that there will be several minor nations. But truly, the greatest reason I am writing this book is not for Americans, but for Japanese.

　この崩壊から生まれるアメリカは、マイナーな国家になるでしょう。私はマイナーな国がいくつか誕生すると予測しています。しかし、私がこの本を書いている最大の理由は、アメリカ人ではなく、日本人に伝えたいことがあるからなのです。

Many Americans are beginning to understand their danger. But I am primarily writing this book for Japanese people. It is still possible to save Japan from being pulled to destruction along with America.

　多くのアメリカ人がその危険性を理解し始めています。しかし、私は主に日本人のためにこの本を書いています。アメリカの破滅に引きずり込まれるであろう日本を救うことは、まだ可能です。

But it will take work.

　しかしそのためには、やらなければならないことがあります。

Introduction
はじめに／3

Chapter 1 Present day America
第1章　現在のアメリカ

The collapse of American cities
アメリカ都市の崩壊……11

Do Left-wing Black Americans ignore crime?
左派黒人だと犯罪が許される？……14

The migrant crisis
不法移民の問題……19

The viciousness of migrant criminals
不法移民の狼藉……21

The destruction of American cities
アメリカ地方都市の惨状……25

Waves of refugees from cities : the rich, the middle class, the poor
都市からの難民の波―富裕層・中産階級・貧困層……32

American cities go extinct
滅亡に向かう地方都市……36

The American Armed Forces in civil war
アメリカ内戦の危険性……45

The severity of race war
深刻な人種対立……53

The elites destroying America
アメリカを破壊するエリートたち……55

The decline of the US military
アメリカ軍の衰退……60

Inferior weapons
劣った武器……69

The militia movement
民兵運動……72

The Migrants
移民たち……75

The Christian Fundamentalists
キリスト教原理主義者（福音派）……77

The Ukraine war, an enormous military and foreign policy disaster
ウクライナ戦争……82

The Ukrainian endgame
ウクライナ戦争の今後……93

The Middle Eastern conflict
中東戦争……95

The bane of America, "Feminism"
諸悪の元凶「フェミニスト」……97

The Feminist destruction of the Education system
フェミニストによる教育破壊……101

The decline of American power
アメリカのマンパワーの劣化……106

American business troubles
アメリカのビジネストラブル……110

The dystopian future of America
ディストピア化するアメリカ……112

Elon Musk's personal tragedy
イーロン・マスクの悲劇……120

Chapter 2 The American future
第2章　アメリカの未来

Donald Trump and the elections
ドナルド・トランプと選挙……124

The criminal cases against Donald Trump
トランプ前大統領に対する裁判……127

The truck drivers strike
トラックドライバーによるストライキ……133

The greed of the Democrats
利己主義を極めるアメリカ民主党……137

The Trump and Biden debate
トランプとバイデンの討論……139

Biden a mere puppet
操り人形・バイデン……143

The Trump assassination attempt
トランプ暗殺未遂事件……147

Biden retires from the race for President
バイデン大統領選から撤退……157

Kamala Harris & Tim Walz
カマラ・ハリスとティム・ウォルツ……160

Robert Kennedy Junior endorses Trump
ロバート・ケネディ・ジュニア、トランプ支持を表明……167

The elections, how will they go?
2024大統領選の見通し……169

Chapter 3 What should Japan do?
第3章 日本は何をすべきか？

First and formost, what not to do.
まず第一に、してはいけないこと……172

The expansion of the Japanese military
日本軍を増強せよ……180

Foreigners in Japan
日本に住む外国人……185

A new foreign policy
外交上の新しい選択肢……189

Concerns about the new prime minister
新首相への不安……195

The nightmare of the 2028 Olympics
2028ロスオリンピックの悪夢……198

Afterword
おわりに／*202*

Chapter 1 Present day America
第1章　現在のアメリカ

The collapse of American cities
アメリカ都市の崩壊

We can now see the general course of American collapse. It is well underway. And I do not think it can be reversed in any reasonable length of time. When I considered the coming American civil war, I originally believed American cities would be blockaded by Right-wing forces, for example,the civilian militias.

　アメリカ崩壊の大まかな流れが見えてきました。それはすでに始まっています。そして、妥当な期間内にそれを覆すことはできないと思います。来るべきアメリカの内戦について考えたとき、私は当初、アメリカの都市は民兵のような右翼勢力によって封鎖されるだろうと考えていました。

It would be quite easy for a militia force to set up a roadblock on an expressway to prevent trucks from moving through. Or to tear up railroad tracks. If such an event happened, local law enforcement and local military units would likely side with the militia forces.

　民兵が高速道路を封鎖してトラックの通行を妨げるのは簡単なことです。あるいは線路を破壊することもできます。もしそのようなことが起これば、地元の警察や軍隊は民兵の側に立つことになるでしょう。

Chapter 1 Present day America

This is because Left-wing governments demonize police forces, and discriminate against White people in the military. As I write this, the new Chief of Staff, General Brown, has declared a hold on all promotions of White male officers in the military.

　左翼政府は警察を悪者扱いし、軍隊では白人を差別しているからです。これを書いている今、新しい参謀総長のブラウン将軍は、軍における白人男性将校の昇進をすべて保留すると宣言しました。

This is definitely going to create many disgruntled White officers. Some may contemplate revolt.

　これは間違いなく、不満を持つ多くの白人将校を生み出すでしょう。反乱を考える者も出てくるでしょう。

However,the election prospects for Donald Trump are surging. As this political crisis between Left and Right has been unfolding in America over the past few decades, the Right has resorted to the rule of law.

　しかし、ドナルド・トランプ氏の選挙の勝算は高まっています。過去数十年にわたり、アメリカでは左派と右派の間で政治的危機が展開される中、右派は法治主義に訴えてきました。

The Left has sought to distort the law in its own favor. So the Right will basically wait for the election. The Left is panicking over the prospect of an election, and I will cover that in a future chapter.

第1章　現在のアメリカ

左派は自分たちに有利なように法律を歪めようとしてきました。右派は基本的に選挙を待ちます。左派は選挙の行方を不安視しています。この点については後で取り上げます。

What is now destroying American cities is primarily the increase in crime. This increase has two causes: the allowance of crime by Leftist government officials, and the reduction of police forces.

今、アメリカの都市を破壊しているのは、主に犯罪の増加です。この増加には二つの原因があります。左派の政府高官による犯罪の容認と、警察力の低下です。

This is affecting all major cities. Boston, New York, Washington DC, Chicago, St. Louis, Los Angeles San Francisco, Portland, and Seattle. And at the same time. America would probably weather the collapse of one or two major cities, but all urban areas at the same time will fundamentally change the structure of America.

これはすべての主要都市に影響を及ぼしています。ボストン、ニューヨーク、ワシントンDC、シカゴ、セントルイス、ロサンゼルス、サンフランシスコ、ポートランド、シアトルです。アメリカは一つか二つの主要都市が崩壊しても乗り切れるでしょうが、すべての都市部が同時に崩壊すれば、アメリカの構造は根本的に変化することでしょう。

Chapter 1 Present day America

Do Left-wing Black Americans ignore crime?
左派黒人だと犯罪が許される？

American liberals wanted to create a better world, a better America. Thinking that traditional America was based on oppression, they felt that if the oppression was removed that a better world would result.

　アメリカのリベラル派は、より良い世界、より良いアメリカを作り出そうとしていました。彼らは、伝統的なアメリカは抑圧の上に成り立っていると考え、抑圧を取り除けばより良い世界が生まれると考えました。

One of the fundamental tenets of this philosophy is that Black people are oppressed. Society needs to be modified. The truth is that Black Americans are 5 times more likely to end up in prison than Whites. Liberals feel that police single out Blacks for more oppressive treatment, resulting in this disparity.

　この哲学の基本理念の一つは、黒人は抑圧されているというものです。社会を修正する必要があります。実際、黒人が刑務所に入る確率は白人の5倍以上です。リベラル派は、警察が黒人をより厳しく扱う対象と見なしているため、このような差が生じていると思っています。

The fact is that Blacks do commit more crime. America has never been able to shed the effects of slavery. America has never been able to get Black Americans into normal society as a group. Immigrants from

Africa do much better than Black Americans, so this is not racial.

　黒人の犯罪が多いのは事実です。アメリカは奴隷制度の余波からいまだに抜け出せていません。アメリカはアメリカ黒人をグループとして一般社会に取り込むことができていません。アフリカからの移民は、アメリカ黒人よりもはるかにうまくやっていますから、単に人種的な問題ではありません。

There are many reasons for this. Primarily, Democratic welfare payments for Black single mothers destroyed Black families. They destroyed the Black society that existed previously. But Left-wing ideology demanded that the Left support single mothers.

　これには多くの理由があります。第一に、黒人シングルマザーに対する民主党の福祉給付が黒人家族を破壊しました。それらは、以前存在していた黒人社会を破壊しました。しかし、左翼のイデオロギーは、左翼がシングルマザーを支援することを要求しました。

Children growing up in families without fathers had no stable male role models growing up, and tended towards a life of crime. The mothers have more children outside of wedlock, and the pattern repeats itself.

　父親のいない家庭で育った子供は、成長過程でしっかりした男性の模範となる人物がいないため、犯罪に手を染める傾向にあります。母親は婚外子を多く産み、このパターンが繰り返されます。

Chapter 1 Present day America

 But Leftists desire sexual freedom for Black women. They claim that men are not necessary in families. They claim that the reasons for crime are the oppression of Black people by society. In particular by the police forces. This is the reason they are attempting to abolish police forces across America.

　しかし、左翼は黒人女性の性的自由を望んでいます。彼らは、家族に男性は必要ないと主張しています。犯罪の原因は社会による黒人への抑圧だと主張しています。特に警察による抑圧です。これが、彼らがアメリカ全土で警察を廃止しようとしている理由です。

Yet in many large cities police departments have had funding cut, since liberal politicians feel that police automatically oppress non-White people. And crime has become decriminalized. There is the famous shoplifting law. Stealing an amount of goods under $950 is now a misdemeanor in most of America.

　多くの大都市では、警察署の予算が削減されています。リベラル派の政治家たちは、警察が自発的に非白人を抑圧していると感じているからです。そして、犯罪が非犯罪化されてしまいました。有名な万引きに関する法律があります。950ドル以下の商品を盗んでも、現在アメリカの大半の地域で大した罪に問われません。

If police arrest a criminal, liberal District Attorneys release them within hours, without bail. So police don't bother to arrest criminals. If the Left-wing District attorney, or the Left-wing media, disapprove of the actions of police, they may be arrested or go to prison.

第1章　現在のアメリカ

　警察が犯罪者を逮捕しても、リベラルな地方検事は保釈金なしで数時間以内に釈放します。だから警察は犯罪者をわざわざ逮捕しません。左翼地方検事や左翼メディアが警察の行動を不服とすれば、警察官が逮捕されるか刑務所に入れられるかもしれません。

An example is former Minneapolis police officer Derek Chauvin. He arrived at a crime scene where George Floyd was using counterfeit money. Mr. Floyd was very difficult to control, as he had a very lethal dose of the drug Fentanyl in his system. Despite officer Chauvin's efforts, Mr. Floyd died from his drug overdose.

　その一例が、ミネアポリスの元警官デレク・ショーヴィン巡査です。彼はジョージ・フロイド氏が偽札を使用した犯行現場に到着しました。彼は致死量のフェンタニルという薬物を摂取していたため、フロイド氏を取り押さえるのは非常に困難でした。ショーヴィン巡査の努力にもかかわらず、フロイド氏は薬物の過剰摂取が原因で死亡しました。

The result was nationwide riots urged on by the Left-wing media. Officer Chauvin was arrested and sent to prison. 200 cities across America had their shopping districts were burned, and more than 30 people died.

　その結果、左翼メディアによって全国的な暴動が引き起こされました。ショーヴィン巡査は逮捕され、刑務所に送られました。全米200の都市で商店街が焼かれ、30人以上が死亡しました。

Chapter 1 Present day America

So crime is now okay if you are what the American Left regards as a repressed minority. Crime has increased greatly. Retail outlets cannot make a profit if people are allowed to steal their goods. In 2023, the Walmart chain closed four stores in Chicago, and two in Portland. Walgreens has closed 27 locations in San Francisco.

　つまり、アメリカの左派が抑圧されたマイノリティと見なす存在であれば、犯罪は許されるようになったのです。犯罪は大幅に増加しています。小売店は、商品を盗むことが許されていては利益を上げることができません。2023年、ウォルマート・チェーンはシカゴで4店舗、ポートランドで2店舗を閉鎖しました。ウォルグリーンはサンフランシスコで27店舗を閉鎖しました。

Homeless man smoking fentanyl (Tenderloin, San Francisco)
フェンタニルを吸うホームレス（サンフランシスコ , テンダーロイン）

第1章 現在のアメリカ

The migrant crisis
不法移民の問題

America has always had illegal immigrants. People crossing into America, without permission. However, under the Biden administration, the numbers have grown astronomically. In the three years of the Biden administration, the number of illegal immigrants has equaled the last ten years before Biden was elected.

　アメリカには常に不法移民がいました。許可なくアメリカに入ってくる人々です。しかし、バイデン政権下でその数は天文学的に増加しました。バイデン政権の3年間で、不法移民の数はバイデン大統領が選出される前の過去10年間と同じになりました。

Why? The Democrats feel that these people will feel gratitude towards the Democratic party, and always vote for Democrats and support their agenda.

　なぜでしょうか？　民主党は、これらの人々が民主党に感謝の念を抱き、常に民主党に投票し、彼らの政策を支持してくれると期待しているからです。

This is a strategic mistake by the Democrats. The migrants are basically Catholic. Thus, they will be basically conservative. They will not support Democratic Party initiatives such as the promotion of LGBT culture in America.

Chapter 1 Present day America

　これは民主党の戦略的ミスです。移民は基本的にカトリック教徒です。したがって、基本的に保守的です。彼らは、アメリカにおけるLGBT文化の促進といった民主党の政策を支持しないでしょう。

Some American politicians have proposed putting these illegal migrants in the military. This is because the US military is facing a drastic lack of volunteers. This would be disastrous. It would create a third force in an America that is facing armed civil conflict, these people would fight for themselves.

　アメリカの政治家の中には、こうした不法移民を軍隊に入れることを提案している者もいます。アメリカ軍が深刻な志願兵不足に直面しているためです。この提案は悲惨な結果をもたらすでしょう。武力衝突に発展しかねない状況下にあるアメリカに、第3の勢力を生み出すことになります。この人たちは自分たちのために戦うでしょう。

Some estimates say around 80% of the migrants are from criminal gangs based in Central and South America. Notable here are the El Salvadorian gang MS-13 and the Venezuelan Tren de Aragua. Operate in the United States, they have formed an alliance and run gangs of looters together.

　移民の約80パーセントは、中南米を拠点とする犯罪組織出身者だとの推計もあります。ここで注目すべきは、エルサルバドルのギャング団MS-13とベネズエラのトレン・デ・アラグアです。両組織はアメリカで提携し、強盗団を共同で運営しています。

The viciousness of migrant criminals
不法移民の狼藉

This process is accelerating. During the Biden administration, approximately 10 million illegal immigrants entered the United States. Many of them are turning to crime. In Oak Brook, a suburb of Chicago, some 47 shoplifters have been arrested. They were all illegal aliens. In New York City, MS-13, a very violent gang from El Salvador, is allying with the Venezuelan gang Tren de Aragua to sell drugs and commit crimes.

　このプロセスは加速しています。バイデン政権時代、約1000万人の不法移民がアメリカに入国しました。その多くが犯罪に手を染めています。シカゴ郊外のオークブルックでは、47人の万引き犯が逮捕されました。彼らはすべて不法滞在者でした。ニューヨークでは、エルサルバドル出身の非常に凶暴なギャング団MS-13が、ベネズエラのギャング団トレン・デ・アラグアと手を組み、ドラッグの販売などの犯罪を行っています。

In February in Chicago, 100 migrants attacked the guards at a Home Depot store in Chicago, the news media did not even report it.

　シカゴでは2月、100人の移民がホーム・デポの店舗で警備員を襲撃しましたが、ニュース・メディアは報道しませんでした。

Los Angeles is plagued by professional thieves from Colombia. They specialize in burglarizing the homes of the rich. They know how to

Chapter 1 Present day America

bypass sophisticated alarm systems. And they are very violent. If they come across residents, they often kill them.

ロサンゼルスはコロンビアから来たプロの窃盗団に悩まされています。彼らは金持ちの家に忍び込むのが専門です。彼らは高度な警報システムを回避する方法を知っています。そして非常に暴力的です。住民に出くわすと、しばしば殺してしまいます。

Some reports estimate the percentage of criminals among the new migrants is 80%.

一部の報道では、新移民に占める犯罪者の割合は80パーセントに達するとされています。

As the cities become uninhabitable, people leave. At present, it is basically the wealthier people, people who have the resources to live in another location. During the riots 2020 after the death of George Floyd, New York City lost some 500,000 people over the three months of the summer.

都市が住めなくなると、人々は去っていきます。現状では、基本的に裕福な人、別の場所で生活できるだけの資産を持つ人々です。ジョージ・フロイド氏の死後に起きた2020年の暴動で、ニューヨーク市の人口は夏の3カ月間で約50万人が流出しました。

These were the most wealthy people, who often possessed homes and villas in other locations. They are not a burden on their destinations.

But they are none the less refugees. The next group of refugees will be the middle class. They will have more trouble finding a place to live, a job in rural areas. After all, a rural town is likely to have enough dentists, and lawyers, so new arrivals will have a hard time finding work.

　彼らは最も裕福な人々で、しばしば他の場所に家や別荘を所有しています。彼らは移住先に負担をかけることはありません。しかし、それでも彼らは難民です。次の難民グループは中産階級です。彼らは地方で住む家や仕事を見つけるのに苦労するでしょう。結局のところ、地方の町には歯科医や弁護士などが十分にいる可能性が高いので、新参者は簡単には仕事を見つけられないでしょう。

The last group of refugees will be the poor. They will not have skills or any economic resources. They will be lucky to find work as manual laborers. They will not have the proper clothes or footwear to survive in the countryside.

　最後の難民グループは貧しい人々です。彼らは技術も経済的余裕もありません。肉体労働者としての仕事が見つかれば幸運です。地方での生活に適した衣服や履物も持っていません。

I was born in Chicago, and I spent my teen aged years in rural Wisconsin. The temperature in winter is around minus 20 to 40 degrees celsius. We often had travelers from warmer states who would die in sudden snowstorms, because they did not have the proper clothing.

Chapter 1 Present day America

　私はシカゴで生まれ、10代をウィスコンシン州の田舎で過ごしました。冬の気温はマイナス20度から40度くらい。暖かい州から来た旅行者が、適切な防寒具を持っていなかったために、突然の吹雪で命を落とすこともよくありました。

Refugees will die in large numbers.

　多くの難民が命を落とすことになるでしょう。

This will also affect the suburbs, as inner-city criminals are already regularly invading the suburbs to commit crimes.

　また、これは郊外にも影響を及ぼすでしょう。すでに都心部の犯罪者が郊外へ侵入し、犯罪を犯すことが日常的に起こっているからです。

There is no political will among radical Liberal politicians to address the issue. Ayanna Pressley, a Congresswoman from Massachusetts, has said that retail outlets are closing because of racism. Mayor Johnson of Chicago has declared if reparations for slavery are paid to Black people, crime will cease. Both of these people are radical Black Leftists.

　急進的なリベラル派の政治家には、この問題に取り組む政治的意志がありません。マサチューセッツ州選出の下院議員アヤナ・プレスリー氏は、人種差別が原因で小売店が閉店していると発言しました。シカゴのジョンソン市長は、奴隷制度に対する賠償金を黒人に

支払えば犯罪はなくなると言明しています。いずれも急進的な黒人左翼です。

In Boston, Black citizens groups are suing Walgreens. A store is closing in their neighborhood. Many of the local citizens are elderly, and will have difficulty going to a more distant location. Yet, the store is closing because of theft. Rather than face the true cause of the problem-crime-they demand ten million dollars from Walgreens.

　ボストンで黒人市民団体がウォルグリーンを提訴しました。彼らの近くにある店舗が閉店します。地元の市民は高齢者が多く、遠い場所に行くのは困難です。しかし、店舗が閉店するのは万引きが原因です。彼らは犯罪という問題の真の原因には向き合わず、ウォルグリーンに1000万ドルの賠償金を要求しているのです。

The destruction of American cities
アメリカ地方都市の惨状

I think it must be the Leftist woke ideology that makes her truly believes there is some other cause for crime. Many of my Japanese friends think of New York being like Tokyo, where Boston is the American Kyoto. But Boston will soon suffer the same destruction and mayhem that plague other American cities.

　犯罪には何か別の原因があると本気で信じているのは、左翼的な覚醒イデオロギーによるものなのでしょう。私の日本人の友人の多くは、ニューヨークは東京のようで、ボストンはアメリカの京都の

Chapter 1 Present day America

ようだと考えています。しかし、ボストンはやがて、他のアメリカの都市を悩ませているのと同じ破壊と騒乱に見舞われるでしょう。

A look at Detroit.

　デトロイトを見てみましょう。

If we look at Detroit, we can get an idea of what the American cities of the future will look like.

　デトロイトを見れば、未来のアメリカの都市がどのようなものになるのかがわかるでしょう。

In the 1950s, Detroit had one million eight hundred thousand people. It was the fourth largest city in the United States. Since then the population has dropped to around 640,000. The cause of this drop was economic. Detroit had one major industry, the automobile manufacturing industry. This industry changed drastically with the adoption of the assembly line.

　1950年代、人口180万人のデトロイト。アメリカ第4の都市でした。その後、人口は約64万人まで減少しました。その原因は経済的なものでした。デトロイトの主要産業は自動車製造業でした。この産業は、組み立てラインの導入によって大きく変化しました。

To have an assembly line, factories need a lot of space. The line could only operate if it was on one level. The factories in the city were multi story operations, and could not physically expand. So they were simply abandoned. Factories were built in the suburbs, and the workers followed. So the old multi story factories, and many homes, were simply abandoned.

組み立てラインを設置するには、工場は広いスペースを必要とします。ラインは1階建てでなければ稼働できません。街の工場は複数階建てで、物理的に拡張することができませんでした。そのため、工場は放棄されました。工場は郊外に建設され、労働者もそこに移りました。そのため、古い複数階建ての工場や多くの住宅は、放棄されたのです。

Today, they stand in ruins. The workers who moved to the suburbs were mostly White. Black workers could not move to the suburbs, as discriminatory real estate practices prevented them from buying homes in the suburbs.

今日、それらは廃墟と化しています。郊外に移り住んだ労働者のほとんどは白人でした。黒人労働者は、差別的な不動産の商慣習により郊外に家を買うことができなかったからです。

So we have a city in ruins. There has been some effort to rebuild the center of the city in recent years. But the majority of the city is in ruins. City services, such as education, police, and the fire department have declined.

そのため、街は荒廃しています。近年、街の中心部を再建しよう

Chapter 1 Present day America

とする努力がなされています。しかし、街の大部分は荒廃したままです。教育、警察、消防といった市の公益業務は劣化しています。

However, this situation of a city full of poor non-White residents gives us an idea of the future of most American urban centers. What we will see is areas denuded of their middle class and upper class residents.

　しかし、白人以外の貧しい住民であふれたこの都市の状況は、アメリカのほとんどの都心部の将来像を示しています。今後、中流階級や上流階級の住民が姿を消した地域を目にすることになるでしょう。

Police will gradually concentrate their efforts to protect the wealthier areas, leaving the poorer areas to fend for themselves. Eventually, these

Drug addicts on the streets of Philadelphia (The woman on the left is holding a syringe)
フィラデルフィアの路上に集う薬物中毒者ら（左側の女性は注射器を手にしている）

efforts will fail; the police will likely disintegrate.

　警察は次第に裕福な地域を守ることに力を注ぐようになり、貧しい地域は自分たちで身を守るしかない状況になっていきます。やがてこうした対応は失敗に終わり、治安維持のための警察組織は崩壊するでしょう。

Retail outlets where sell food are leaving cities due to high crime. Left-wing District Attorneys are refusing to prosecute people who rob and loot. Some people claim it is because Black people have been historically oppressed; others say that previous oppression gives Black people the right to loot and riot today.

　食品を購入できる小売店は、犯罪が多いために都市から次々と撤退しています。左翼の地方検事は、強盗や略奪を働いた人々を起訴することを拒否しています。それらの犯罪が起きるのは、黒人が歴史的に抑圧されてきたからだと主張する人もいますし、過去の抑圧が今日の黒人に略奪や暴動をする権利を与えているのだと言う人もいます。

The next city to collapse will be Baltimore. The Left-wing city council has made extreme cuts to the police budget. A district of 61,000 people is patrolled by three officers. Calls for police assistance go unanswered.

　次に崩壊する都市はボルチモアでしょう。左翼市議会は警察予算を大幅に削減しました。人口6万1000人の地区を巡回するのは、3

人の警官です。警察への通報にも応答しません。

Baltimore has many problems, the sewerage system is antiquated, the school system cannot produce any student that reads or can do math at grade level, but city administrators continue to deny that this can be a cause of crime.

　ボルチモアには多くの問題があります。下水道システムは時代遅れで、学校制度はその学年相応の読み書きや計算ができる生徒を一人も輩出できていません。しかし、市の行政当局は、これが犯罪の原因となる可能性を否定し続けています。

They continue to blame cultural factors, such as racial prejudice. Chicago is much the same. The mayor, as I write this, is Brandon Johnson. He is a former professor and a radical Black activist. Rather than focus on crime as a problem, his ideology forces him to consider crime as the result of social troubles, such as racial prejudice.

　彼らは、人種的偏見などの文化的要因が問題であると非難し続けています。シカゴも同じです。これを書いている今、シカゴ市長はブランドン・ジョンソン氏です。彼は元教授で、急進的な黒人活動家でもあります。彼のイデオロギーは、犯罪を問題として取り上げるよりも、人種的偏見などの社会的な問題の結果として犯罪を考えるべきだというものです。

Retail food stores, along with other stores, have left the city in large numbers. There are really almost no major food stores left in urban

第1章　現在のアメリカ

Chicago, residents must travel long distances to find food.

　食料品店をはじめ、多くの店舗がシカゴから撤退しました。シカゴ市内には大手食料品店がほぼ皆無となり、住民は食料品を買うために長距離の移動を余儀なくされています。

Brandon Johnson

 (Chicago Mayor)

ブランドン・ジョンソン
（シカゴ市長）

The mayor's solution is to establish city-run food stores. But this will take money, and expertise that the city does not have. The result will be the same. Criminals will rob these city-run stores.

　市長の解決策は、市が運営する食料品店を設立することです。しかし、これには市にはない資金とノウハウが必要です。しかし結果は同じで、犯罪者はこうした市が運営する店舗を襲うでしょう。

He simply cannot comprehend that stronger police forces are needed to control crime in the city.

　彼は、街の犯罪を抑制するためには、より強力な警察力が必要だということが理解できません。

Waves of refugees from cities : the rich, the middle class, the poor
都市からの難民の波─富裕層・中産階級・貧困層

There will be three basic waves of refugees. The rich are already leaving. They will have homes to go to in rural areas and will be able to support themselves.

　難民には基本的に三つの波があります。富裕層はすでに去っています。彼らは地方に家があり、そこで自活できます。

Next will be the middle class. Most of them will be able to find some employment and housing, however some will not.

　次は中産階級です。彼らの大半は何らかの仕事と住居を確保できるでしょうが、そうでない人もいます。

The third wave will be the urban poor. They will have no employable skills. They will have no transportation. The young people will be armed and violent. Elderly and poor children will simply not be able to leave urban centers, they will most likely die in them.

　第3の波は都市部の貧困層です。彼らは雇用可能なスキルを持ちません。交通手段もありません。若者たちは武装し、暴力的になります。高齢者や貧困層の子供たちは、都心から離れることができず、その中で命を落とす可能性が高いでしょう。

Americans are very obese. Some 66% of Americans are seriously overweight. They simply will not be able to perform any kind of physical work.

　そしてアメリカ人は非常に肥満です。アメリカ人の約66パーセントが深刻な肥満です。彼らは、どんな肉体労働もこなせないでしょう。

These people are not international refugees, but internal American displaced people.

　これらの人々は国際的な難民ではなく、アメリカ国内の避難民です。

This is a very dystopian view. However, rural communities will have no means of supporting large numbers of refugees. In states that traditionally vote Democratic, the big cities are liberal, while rural areas tend to be conservative.

　これは非常に悲観的な見方です。しかし、地方のコミュニティは大量の難民を支援する手段を持ちません。伝統的に民主党に投票する州では、大都市はリベラルで、地方は保守的な傾向があります。

They are refusing to house illegal migrants at the present time. The waves of armed young people will tend to be Black or Hispanic. As I wrote, they will be armed. Suburban police forces are small; therefore, local militias will supplement these local law enforcement organizations.

Chapter 1 Present day America

　彼らは現在、不法移民の収容を拒否しています。武装した若者の波は、黒人かヒスパニック系に多いでしょう。私が書いたように、彼らは武装するでしょう。郊外の警察力は弱いです。だから、地元の民兵がこうした地元の法執行組織を補うことになります。

Racially, this urban population of third wave refugees will be Black and Hispanic people. They will be poor. Outside of northern cities like Chicago, there are few such people in the suburbs, and almost none in rural areas. They will not be well received by the local, primarily white population.

　人種的には、この都市部に住む第3波の難民の多くは黒人やヒスパニック系です。彼らは貧しい人々です。シカゴのような北部の都市を除けば、郊外にはそのような人々はほとんどいませんし、地方にはほぼ皆無です。彼らは基本的に白人の地元住民に受け入れられることはないでしょう。

The result will be hundreds of small battles across America. This is already beginning. As retail stores leave the big cities, criminal gangs in those cities are beginning to raid suburban shopping malls. So far, militias are not being used to protect them.

　その結果、アメリカ全土で何百もの小規模な戦いが起こるでしょう。これはすでに始まっています。小売店が大都市から撤退し、その都市の犯罪組織が郊外のショッピングモールを襲撃し始めています。今のところ、それらのショッピングモールを守るために民兵が動員されていません。

Also in northern America, winters are harsh. Temperatures drop to minus 20 degrees Celsius or more. Even now, weather kills people. These refugees are unlikely to have proper footwear or clothing to survive such difficult weather conditions.

　また、アメリカ北部の冬は厳しいです。気温は摂氏マイナス20度以下まで下がります。今でも天候が原因で命を落とす人がいます。難民たちは、このような厳しい気象条件を生き抜くための適切な履物や衣服を持っている可能性は低いでしょう。

But in the 2020 riots, militias were employed and paid to protect small local businesses, such as bars. Militias did patrol some local suburban towns as organized volunteers. During the 2020 riots, Black

American stores closed by crime

犯罪により閉鎖されたアメリカの店舗

Lives Matter and Antifa robbed and burned some 200 urban shopping districts across American cities. Those protected by militias were not attacked.

　しかし、2020年の暴動では、民兵はバーなどの地元の小さな企業を守るために雇われ、報酬を得ていました。民兵は組織化されたボランティアとして郊外のいくつかの町をパトロールしていました。2020年の暴動では、ブラック・ライブズ・マターとアンティファがアメリカの都市部の商店街約200カ所を襲い、掠奪、放火を行いました。民兵に守られた商店街は攻撃を受けませんでした。

American cities go extinct
滅亡に向かう地方都市

There is another factor to consider. That is serious diseases. In urban homeless encampments, bubonic plague and typhus have reappeared. Among the new migrants, measles has appeared.

　もう一つ考慮すべき要素があります。それは深刻な病気です。都市部のホームレスキャンプでは、ペストやチフスが発生しています。新たな移民の間では、はしかが発生しています。

Can American cities be fixed?

　アメリカの都市は立て直せるでしょうか？

I do not think so. Most large US cities are ruled by Left-wing governments. These governments have shown an amazing inability to learn from their mistakes. The mayor of Chicago has said that they will take in 700,000 more illegal migrants. This is insane. They cannot take care of the people who are already there.

私はそうは思いません。アメリカのほとんどの大都市は左翼政権に支配されています。これらの政府は、自分たちの過ちから学ぶ能力に驚くほど欠けているのです。シカゴ市長は、さらに70万人の不法移民を受け入れると述べています。これは正気の沙汰ではありません。すでに受け入れた人々の面倒を見ることもできないというのに。

So what we are likely to see in the coming American conflict is not the movement of great armies like the civil war of 1861 to 1865, but rather a serious of small guerrilla type actions in the suburbs of major cities. On the side of the suburbs will some police and militia units, on the side of cities will be criminal gangs increasingly desperate for food.

つまり、今後アメリカで起きる紛争で見られるのは、1861〜1865年の南北戦争のような大規模な軍隊の動きではなく、大都市近郊での小規模なゲリラ戦闘の頻発なのです。郊外側には警察や民兵部隊が、都市側には食糧不足でますます困窮する犯罪者集団がいます。

I see two possibilities for the future of America. One that surviving America will be a primarily rural nation. Let us assume that it is led

Chapter 1 Present day America

by Texas. Recently some 25 interior and southern states supported Texas in its efforts to curb illegal immigration into the United States. These states could be an independent nation. They might even still call themselves the "United States of America".

　私はアメリカの将来について二つの可能性があると見ています。一つは、生き残ったアメリカが農村部を中心とした国家になることです。テキサスがそれを主導すると仮定しましょう。最近、内陸部と南部の25州ほどが、アメリカへの不法移民を阻止しようとするテキサス州の取り組みを支持しました。これらの州は独立国家となる可能性があります。その国を引き続き「アメリカ合衆国」と呼称するかもしれません。

The areas around the ruined cities would become "no-go" zones. These zones would extend some 50 or so kilometers outside major urban centers. Transport routes would be rerouted around these ruined cities. But as long as there is electric power, life in this new nation would be much like the America of the 1960's.

　廃墟となった都市の周辺は「立ち入り禁止」区域となります。この区域は、主要都市の中心部から50キロほど離れたところまで広がります。交通ルートはこれらの廃墟と化した都市を迂回することになります。しかし、電力さえあれば、この新国家での生活は1960年代のアメリカとほとんど変わらないでしょう。

It would be a much reduced nation. Of the present population, some 40% just would not survive. Let us call this "America A"

第1章　現在のアメリカ

　この国家は大幅に縮小するでしょう。現在の人口のうち、40パーセントは生き残れないでしょう。これを「アメリカA」と呼びましょう。

Now what we would call "America B". Many people do not realize that America is facing an intense science and engineering crisis. For some 30 years or more, Leftists have dominated education in America. Only in the last recent 5 years there has been an explosion in LGBT and Black studies.

　さて、私たちが「アメリカB」と呼ぶものについてです。多くの人々は、アメリカが科学や工学の分野において危機的状況に直面していることに気づいていません。アメリカでは30年以上にわたって、左翼が教育を支配してきました。LGBTや黒人問題を扱う学問が爆発的に発展したのは、ここ5年ほどのことです。

In America A, most American cities will become no go zones ruled by criminal gangs, if any people live there at all. In rural areas, civilization will still survive. In America B, the national population will be reduced by 90%, people will survive as hunter gathers, transportation will be by horse, all civilization will be lost.

　アメリカAでは、ほとんどのアメリカの都市は、人が住んでいるとしても、犯罪組織に支配された立ち入り禁止区域になります。田舎では、文明はまだ生き残ります。アメリカBでは、国の人口が90パーセント減少し、人々は狩猟採集で生き残り、交通手段は馬となり、すべての文明は失われます。

Chapter 1 Present day America

Long before that, there was an obsession with reducing math and science studies. Feminist groups called these subjects as having been invented by "dead old White men". They felt that this description somehow indicated that these subjects were not worth teaching, or teaching in detail.

　ずっと以前から、数学と科学の授業時間を減らすことに執着する人たちがいました。フェミニスト団体は、これらの科目を「この世にいない過去の白人男性」が発明したものと呼びました。彼らのこの表現は、これらの科目は教える価値がない、あるいは詳しく教える価値がないと考えていることを示しています。

The result of this has been few Americans are qualified in science and math. Until now, the majority of scientists in America, some 60%, are not Americans. The results of this are beginning to show. In the recent Ukraine war, American weapons were across the board inferior to those designed by Russia.

　その結果、科学や数学に精通したアメリカ人は大幅に減少しました。現在、アメリカの科学者の大半、約60パーセントはアメリカ人ではありません。その影響はすでに現れ始めています。最近のウクライナ戦争では、アメリカの兵器はロシア製のものより全体的に劣っていました。

American transit systems are poorly designed and maintained. Well, American companies do not invest in maintenance, they prefer to cut costs to maintain high profits. The same can said for electric power transmission.

　アメリカの交通システムは設計もメンテナンスも不十分です。アメリカの企業はメンテナンスにコストをかけず、高収益を維持するためにコスト削減を優先します。送電についても同じことが言えます。

And foreign engineers and scientists are beginning to return to their native countries. Crime has greatly increased in America, it is not safe to raise a family. Political chaos and civil war are on the horizon. So they go back to China or India.

　また、外国人技術者や科学者が母国に戻り始めています。アメリカでは犯罪が激増し、家族を養うには安全ではありません。政治的な混乱と内戦が目前に迫っています。だから、彼らは中国やインドに帰ります。

The Texas electrical grid is very fragile. There have been several close calls, where the entire grid came close to complete collapse due to weather events. In several cases, engineers were able to craft a solution just minutes before collapse. In the future, there will be fewer and fewer engineers able to maintain power systems.

　テキサスの電力網は非常に脆弱です。悪天候により電力網全体が完全に崩壊しかけた危機的状況は、これまでに何度も発生しています。いくつかの事例では、エンジニアが崩壊の寸前に解決策を見出すことができました。今後、電力網を維持できるエンジニアはますます少なくなるでしょう。

Also, while Texas is basically a conservative state, there are many liberals in the state government and university system. In any potential new independent country, they would be a problem.

また、テキサスは基本的には保守的な州ですが、州政府や大学機関にはリベラル派が多数います。新しい独立国ができた場合、彼らは厄介な存在となるでしょう。

If the Texas grid collapses, it will be for an extended time, perhaps forever. In this case, life in America will be reduced to a subsistence level, something like in medieval Europe. The primary transport system will be by horse.

もしテキサス州の電力網が崩壊すれば、それは長期にわたり、おそらく永続するでしょう。その場合、アメリカでの生活は中世ヨーロッパのような自給自足のレベルにまで落ち込むでしょう。主要な交通手段は馬になります。

Most Americans will not survive this, and America will become a wilderness wasteland.

ほとんどのアメリカ人はその状況で生き残れず、アメリカは荒涼とした荒野と化すでしょう。

Many Japanese people have a hard time understanding this leniency towards criminals. Well, I was born in America, and I have seen intelligent people take political positions that are ridiculous. Americans prefer to force others to adopt their opinions, even if those opinions are dangerous or wrong.

　多くの日本人には、このような犯罪者に対する寛容さは理解し難い問題です。私はアメリカで生まれ育ちましたが、知的な人々がとんでもない政治的主張をするのを目の当たりにしてきました。アメリカ人は、たとえその意見が危険なものであっても、間違ったものであっても、他人に自分の意見を強制することを好みます。

They desire notoriety for forcing those dangerous ideas, and do not care about the damage they cause. For these Americans the power they gain from forcing others to submit is addictive. So the result is that we have a group of people that are in effect promoting crime in American cities, protecting criminals, and preventing police from doing their jobs effectively.

　彼らはそうした危険な考えを強要することで有名になることを望みますが、それが引き起こす被害など気にも留めません。こうしたアメリカ人は、他人に服従を強いることで得られる権力に病みつきになります。その結果、事実上アメリカの都市で犯罪を助長し、犯罪者を擁護し、警察が効果的に職務を遂行するのを妨げている集団が生まれています。

However, recently the mayors of San Francisco, Los Angeles and San Diego have made moves to dismantle proposition 47, which is the called shop lifting law, which decriminalized thefts under $950.

Chapter 1 Present day America

しかし、最近、サンフランシスコ、ロサンゼルス、サンディエゴの各市長は、950ドル以下の窃盗を非犯罪化する第47号議案(いわゆる「万引き法」)を廃止する動きを見せています。

The have recognized that this law has turned their cities into areas full of crime and disease, and that people and businesses are fleeing California.

彼らは、この法律が自分たちの都市を犯罪と病気の蔓延する地域へと変え、人々や企業がカリフォルニアから逃げ出していることを認識しています。

They are opposed by an activist group called "Equality California" , which helped create this law. It originated some 20 years ago as an LGBT group, and decided to reform the California justice system. These people have received donations from celebrities, and received state grants.

これに反対しているのは、この法律の制定に貢献した「イクオリティ・カリフォルニア」という活動家グループです。この団体は20年ほど前にLGBTの団体として発足し、カリフォルニア州の司法制度を改革することを決意しました。彼らは著名人から寄付を受け、州から助成金を受けています。

They will obviously strongly oppose any effort to repeal the "shoplifting law". Unless liberals actually experience crime themselves, they persist in their fantasies that police are evil, and that people commit crime because of social oppression.

　彼らが「万引き法」の撤廃に強く反対するのは、いうまでもありません。リベラル派の人々は実際に自分が犯罪の被害者にならない限り、警察は悪であり、人々が犯罪を犯すのは社会的抑圧のせいだという幻想を抱き続けます。

The mayor of Los Angeles is seeking to hire a few hundred new police officers. This is not enough. Ten thousand of more would be needed. To truly clean up the city, a year or more of martial law would be necessary.

　ロサンゼルス市長は数百人の警察官を新たに雇用しようとしています。これでは足りません。数万人必要でしょう。本当に街を浄化するには、1年以上もの戒厳令の発令が必要でしょう。

The American Armed Forces in civil war
アメリカ内戦の危険性

What role would the armed forces take in such chaos? I see them as taking some part in police work, or perhaps food delivery to areas that have no retail outlets to buy food. However, due to pressure by Left-wing advocates to force politically correct doctrine on the armed forces, I do not see them as capable in such activities.

　このような混乱の中で軍隊はどのような役割を求められるので

Chapter 1 Present day America

しょうか？ それは警察業務の一部や、食料を販売する小売店のない地域への食料供給などです。しかし、政治的に正しい教義を軍に強制しようとする左翼擁護者からの圧力があるため、私は軍隊にそのような活動ができるとは思えません。

The Conservative militia units will basically remain in their communities, and protect them as best as they can. The militia are a potential Right army, but they are divided into many groups. They would need a powerful leader to unite them.

　保守の民兵部隊は基本的に地域社会に留まり、できる限り地域社会を守ります。民兵は潜在的に右派の軍ですが、多くのグループに分かれています。彼らを団結させるには強力なリーダーが必要でしょう。

In the cities, Black and Hispanic groups will form their own gangs, which will be very violent. Suburbs around a city will experience violent attacks from such gangs for a radius of some 30 kilometers from urban areas. These urban gangs will not be to operate well beyond 30 kilometers or so from a city. Gradually, fuel will become scarce in the cities, Then raids of the suburbs will be conducted on foot.

　都市では黒人とヒスパニック系のグループが独自のギャング団を結成し、非常に暴力的になるでしょう。都市近郊では、都市部から半径約 30 キロメートルの範囲で、こうしたギャング団による暴力的な攻撃が発生します。こうした都市部のギャング団は、都市から 30 キロメートル以上離れた場所で活動することはできません。都

市では徐々に燃料が不足し、郊外の襲撃は徒歩で行われるようになります。

Present radical groups like Black Lives Matter or Antifa will simply disappear in the chaos.

　ブラック・ライブズ・マターやアンティファのような現在の過激派グループは、混乱の中で消えていくでしょう。

If in the future we have a country, like "America A" led by perhaps Texas, airports and port facilities near major cities may become unusable. This will due to criminal activity. It is already happening. The Union Pacific railroad is already suffering a large number of attacks on rail borne shipping containers at rail choke point in Los Angeles. The trains must move slowly as they enter the train yard. Thieves simply walk up and break into the containers, strewing the contents all about.

　将来、テキサス州を中心とする「アメリカＡ」のような国が誕生すれば、主要都市近くの空港や港湾施設が使用できなくなる可能性があります。その原因は犯罪行為です。それはすでに起こっています。ユニオン・パシフィック鉄道は、ロサンゼルスの鉄道の要所で輸送コンテナを積んだ貨車が何度も攻撃されています。列車は操車場に入るときに速度を落とさなければなりません。泥棒はただ歩いてコンテナに近づき、侵入して中身を周囲にばらまきます。

Moving trade operations into new airports and seaports will take time. In places like California, nearly all the decent locations are very

Chapter 1 Present day America

close to major urban centers, California in the future will not be very survivable. For a trading nation like Japan, America will be basically cut off.

　貿易業務を新しい空港や港に移すには時間がかかります。カリフォルニアのような場所では、好適な立地のほとんどが大都市中心部に非常に近いところにあるため、将来的にカリフォルニアは生き残りが難しくなるでしょう。日本のような貿易立国にとって、アメリカは基本的に閉ざされた国になります。

As I write this, student protests are sweeping the nation. They are still basically on campus. However, they have expanded to blocking bridges and access to airports.

　私がこれを書いている今、学生運動が全米に広がっています。彼らは基本的にはキャンパス内に集まっていますが、その活動は橋や空港へのアクセスを遮断するまでに拡大しています。

The protests are against support for Israel by universities. For many years, Israel has been waging some type of conflict to gradually push Palestinian people out of Palestine. The fact is the America political world is dominated by rich Jewish people who donate lavishly to both political parties.

　抗議活動は大学によるイスラエル支援に反対するものです。イスラエルは長年にわたり、パレスチナ人を徐々にパレスチナから追い出すために何らかの紛争を起こしてきました。実際のところ、アメ

第 1 章　現在のアメリカ

リカの政界は両政党に多額の献金をする裕福なユダヤ人によって支配されています。

However in the 2024 election, Arab Americans have stood up. They are traditionally Democrat. So Arab Americans are demanding the US government put pressure on Israel. This puts the present Biden administration in an impossible situation.

　しかし、2024年の選挙ではアラブ系アメリカ人が立ち上がりました。彼らは伝統的に民主党支持者です。そのためアラブ系アメリカ人はアメリカ政府に対しイスラエルに圧力をかけるよう要求しています。これにより、現在のバイデン政権は苦境に立たされています。

The Israeli government demands unconditional American support. Yet a large number of Americans are demanding that America punish Israel. Obviously, the Biden administration cannot satisfy both demands.

　イスラエル政府はアメリカに無条件の支援を要求しています。しかし、多くのアメリカ人はアメリカがイスラエルを罰することを要求しています。当然ながら、バイデン政権は両方の要求を満たすことができません。

Recently, after a couple of weeks, this protest movement has been taken over by professional Leftist revolutionaries. This is the Black Lives Matter and Antifa type of people. The Democratic party and American establishment created these groups to attack America and drive Donald Trump from power in the 2020 election.

Chapter 1 Present day America

　数週間後、この抗議運動はプロの左翼革命家に引き継がれました。これはブラック・ライブズ・マターやアンティファなどに所属する人々です。民主党とアメリカの支配層は、アメリカを攻撃し、2020年の選挙でドナルド・トランプ氏を権力の座から追い出すために、これらのグループを創設しました。

After the death of of George Floyd due to a drug overdose, they burned the business districts of some 200 American cities. But they did not simply disband. They continued to exist. Now, they are taking over the pro Palestinian protest movement.

　ジョージ・フロイド氏が薬物の過剰摂取で亡くなった後、彼らはアメリカの約200都市のビジネス街を焼き払いました。彼らは消えたわけではありません。彼らは存在し続けています。今、彼らは親パレスチナ派の抗議運動を掌握しようとしています。

This is a very serious issue for the American Democratic party. These people simply desire destruction. They have no clear idea of what kind of America they wish to create. They represent another side in thee ongoing American civil conflict.

　これはアメリカ民主党にとって非常に深刻な問題です。この人たちはただ破壊を望んでいるのです。彼らはどのようなアメリカを作りたいのか、明確な考えを持っていません。彼らは現在アメリカで起きている内戦の、一方の側を代表しています。

第1章　現在のアメリカ

Many of my Japanese friends have a difficult time understanding this. Do these people not realize that they stand to destroy the country they live in? It is like setting fire to your house, while you sit in the living room watching television.

　私の日本人の友人の多くは、この状況を理解し難いと言います。このアメリカ人たちは自分たちが住んでいる国を破壊していることに気づいていないのでしょうか？　それは、居間でテレビを見ながら、自分の家に火をつけているようなものなのに。

No, like most Americans, these people are very poorly educated and intellectually lazy. They cannot realize they are destroying their own living space.

　ほとんどのアメリカ人がそうなのですが、これらの人々は教育レベルも低く、知的にも怠惰です。彼らは自分たちの生活空間を破壊していることに気づいていません。

So the American civil conflict that is arising is quite multi sided. There are the Democrats versus Republicans, Radical Black people demanding special rights, large numbers of violent South American illegal migrants who are already creating criminal empires in America, and now there are professional violent Left-wing groups.

　つまり、今アメリカで起きている内戦は、非常に多面的なものなのです。民主党と共和党の対立、特別な権利を要求する急進的な黒人、すでにアメリカで犯罪ネットワークを築きつつある多数の暴力

Chapter 1 Present day America

的な南米からの不法移民、そして、プロの暴力的な左翼グループもいます。

In fact, the criminal looting gangs are expanding their operations. Gangs from New York City are now looting throughout the East coast, all the way down to Washington DC. They then sell the goods in New York City. However Manhattan District Attorney Alvin Bragg spends a lot of time prosecuting Donald Trump on fanciful politically motivated charges, but does not prosecute looters at all.

　実際、強盗団はその活動を拡大しています。ニューヨーク市のギャング団は現在、ワシントンDCに至る東海岸で略奪を行っており、その略奪品をニューヨーク市で販売しています。しかし、マンハッタン地方検事のアルビン・ブラッグ氏は、政治的動機に基づく荒唐無稽な容疑でドナルド・トランプ氏を起訴することに多くの時間を費やしていますが、強盗団についてはまったく起訴していません。

I have written that this is evidence that US cities are declining rapidly into advanced decay. Presidential candidate Donald Trump has declared that he will deport all illegal aliens if elected. Well, this sounds good as election rhetoric, but is it practically possible? He has said that he will use the military to do it if necessary.

　これはアメリカの都市が急速に荒廃しつつある証拠であると私は書きました。大統領候補ドナルド・トランプ氏は、当選したらすべての不法滞在者を国外追放すると宣言しました。まあ、これは選挙のスローガンとしてはよいフレーズですが、実際にそれは可能で

しょうか？　同氏は必要なら軍を使ってでもそれを実行すると述べました。

It will be necessary. States will not have the law enforcement personnel to do it. But the US military is 17% Hispanic. These troops will be very reluctant to arrest people who are of the same ethnic group, religion and language.

　それは必要になります。各州にはそれを行う法執行職員がいないでしょう。しかし、アメリカ軍にはヒスパニック系が17パーセントいます。同じ民族であり、同じ宗教、言語をもつ人々を逮捕することに、これらの部隊は非常に消極的になるでしょう。

The severity of race war
深刻な人種対立

Speaking of a lack of law enforcement personnel, recently there was a case in Chicago, where two armed men entered a woman's home. She called the police. It was four hours before they arrived. There simply are not enough police.

　法執行機関の人員不足について言えば、最近シカゴで武装した男2人が女性宅に押し入った事件がありました。彼女は警察に通報しましたが、警察が到着するまでに4時間かかりました。警察官が圧倒的に不足しているのです。

Chapter 1 Present day America

Yet the mayor of Chicago is a radical Marxist, he is convinced that the police are the cause of social problems. He will not increase their numbers.

しかし、シカゴ市長は過激なマルクス主義者であり、警察が社会問題の元凶だと確信しています。彼は警察官を増員することはないでしょう。

This cannot work well. Also, race relations between Black Americans and White Americans are now terrible. Because of Left-wing policies, they are extremely hostile to one another.

これではうまくいくはずがありません。また、黒人アメリカ人と白人アメリカ人の間の人種関係は現在、最悪の状態です。左翼政策により、両者は互いに激しい敵意を抱いています。

But the Hispanics are quiet, simply living their lives. Any action by a future President Trump, to arrest illegal aliens that are mostly Hispanic, will greatly anger the Hispanic population, and force them into becoming another hostile group in America.

ヒスパニック系の人たちは静かに、ただ自分たちの生活を送っています。将来トランプ大統領が、ヒスパニック系が大部分を占める不法滞在者を検挙するという行動をとれば、ヒスパニック系住民は大いに怒り、アメリカ国内での新たな敵対的集団となるでしょう。

第1章 現在のアメリカ

The elites destroying America
アメリカを破壊するエリートたち

When I talk to many Japanese people about American troubles, Japanese people often ask how they can help America. This is not my intention in giving speeches or writing books. I am trying to tell Japanese people we must save Japan.

　私が多くの日本人にアメリカの問題について話すと、日本人はよく「アメリカを助けるにはどうすればよいですか」と尋ねてきます。それは、私が講演したり本を書いたりする意図ではありません。私は日本人に、日本を救わなければならないと言いたいのです。

What people in Japan do not understand is that the American troubles are deliberate. They are created by the American elite. That is, wealthy White Americans, primarily from the Northeast and West coast of the United States. These people believe themselves to be specially privileged, and that they have greater rights than most people.

　日本の人々が理解していないのは、アメリカの問題は意図的に起こされているということです。それらはアメリカのエリート層によって作り出されているのです。つまり、主にアメリカ北東部と西海岸出身の裕福な白人アメリカ人です。これらの人々は、自分たちは特権階層であり、一般の人よりも大きな権利があると信じています。

Of course, they will not think of anything beneficial for Japan. They look at Japan as a subservient country, that owes America a great debt.

This of course is not true at all. But they only call on Japan when they want financing for some thing, usually covering American mistakes.

　もちろん、彼らは日本の利益など考えることはありません。彼らは日本を、アメリカに尽くすべき従属国と見なしています。もちろん、これはまったく間違った考えです。彼ら何かのために資金が必要になると、日本に提供を要請します。たいていはアメリカの過ちを尻拭いさせるためです。

That is why they are requesting money to cover the Ukrainian war. That money is simply going to the American MIC, or Military Industrial Complex.

　そういうわけで、彼らはウクライナ戦争の費用をまかなうために、その資金を日本に要求しています。その資金はアメリカのＭＩＣ、すなわち軍産複合体に流れるだけです。

But these elite people are now intent on destroying America. People like this are behind the open borders, which bring in so many illegal aliens. They feel superior to Americans who live in the Heartland of America, and wish to replace people of the Heartland with new immigrants.

　しかし、これらのエリートたちは今、アメリカを破壊することに熱心です。このような人々が、多くの不法移民を受け入れる国境開放政策の背後にいます。彼らはアメリカのハートランド（アメリカの伝統的価値観が支配的な地域）に住むアメリカ人に対して優越感

を抱いており、ハートランドの人々を新しい移民に置き換えること
を望んでいます。

They have some vague idea that people of the Heartland will simply disappear. Then the new immigrants will replace them at a cheaper wage. This is incredibly naive, but these people have political power now in the United States, in the Biden administration.

　彼らは、ハートランドの人々はこれから消え去っていくという漠然とした考えを持っています。より安い賃金で働く新しい移民が彼らに取って代わるだろうと考えているのです。これは信じられないほど単純な考えですが、これらの人々は現在、バイデン政権下のアメリカにおいて政治的な力を持っています。

Japanese people are incredibly kind, and have a very difficult time understanding this. Most Americans believe that the United States government is their enemy. And they are correct. The government does not regard the welfare of the America people as its responsibility. Instead, they work for the profit of various corporations that contribute to the campaigns of politicians.

　日本人は信じられないほど親切ですが、そんな日本人には、このことを理解するのは非常に困難です。ほとんどのアメリカ人はアメリカ政府が自分たちの敵だと信じています。そしてそれは正しいのです。政府はアメリカ国民の福祉を政府の責任とは考えていません。彼らは国民の方を向いておらず、政治家の選挙活動に貢献するさまざまな企業の利益のために働いています。

Chapter 1 Present day America

At best, the political class ignores the normal people, at worst, they do harm to them. This can be clearly seen in the importation of millions of illegal aliens to replace normal American workers.

　政治家は一般の国民に対して、良くて放置、悪ければ害を及ぼします。これは、一般のアメリカ人労働者に取って代わる、何百万もの不法移民を流入させている事実からも明らかです。

When Japanese people meet average Americans, they are often friendly and kind. What they do not realize is that people change when they enter a major corporation or government. Their hearts are corrupted by greed, and they turn to evil.

　日本人が一般的なアメリカ人に会うと、彼らの多くは友好的で親切です。日本人が気づいていないのは、大企業や政府に入ると人は変わるということです。彼らの心は欲によって腐敗し、悪に染まるのです。

The creation of this class of elite people has been going on for decades. Recently, there have been extensive protests against American support for Israel in its war on Palestinian people in Gaza. American students occupied Hamilton Hall in Columbia University in New York City. A student spokesperson, Johannah King-Slutzky, demanded that the school supply the students with food and water while they occupied the Hall.

　このようなエリート層の形成は何十年も続いています。最近、ガザ地区のパレスチナ人に対する戦争で、アメリカのイスラエル支援

に対して大規模な抗議活動が起きています。ニューヨーク市のコロンビア大学では、ハミルトンホールをアメリカ人学生が占拠しました。学生の広報担当者、ヨハンナ・キング・スルツキー氏は、学生たちがホールを占拠している間、学校側が学生たちに食料と水を提供するよう要求しました。

She felt it was their right as Humanitarian aid. In this age of the internet, this young woman instantly became nationally famous. As a selfish idiot. And she is on course to becoming an elite American. It is a shame.

彼女は、人道的配慮としてそれが当然の権利であると感じていました。このインターネット時代において、この若い女性は瞬く間に全国的に有名になりました。利己的な愚か者として。そして彼女はエリートアメリカ人への道を進んでいます。残念です。

But to Japanese people, we cannot help America in such a situation. Americans will have to handle this problem themselves. It is a civil war. If we try to help, we only make enemies of one side or the other, and be pulled into the war. In Japan, we can only step back, and hope that Americans can solve their domestic problems without too much violence.

しかし、日本人としては、このような状況ではアメリカを助けることはできません。アメリカ人は自分たちでこの問題に対処しなければなりません。これは内戦なのです。私たちが助けようとしても、どちらか一方を敵に回し、戦争に巻き込まれるだけです。日本では、

私たちは一歩下がって、アメリカ人があまり暴力的な手段を使わず、この国内問題を解決することを願うしかありません。

The decline of the US military
アメリカ軍の衰退

I am sometimes amazed at how many people believe in the American military. American people have become disillusioned in recent years, the American military is no longer respected like it once was.

アメリカ軍を信じている人がいかに多いかということに、私は時々驚かされます。近年、アメリカ人は幻滅し、アメリカ軍はかつてのように尊敬されなくなりました。

Americans no longer believe in the American military. It has been too politicized. Japanese people do not know the true state of the military, and still believe it is functional enough to defend Japan. This is not so.

アメリカ人はもはやアメリカ軍を信じていない。あまりにも政治化されすぎているからです。日本人はアメリカ軍の本当の状態を知らず、いまだに日本を守るのに十分機能していると思っています。しかし、そうではありません。

Left-wing activists have specifically targeted the military. When Barack Obama became President in January of 2009, one of the first things he did was fire some 197 officers of the United States military, from

General and Admiral ranks down to Lieutenant Colonels. The reason was that he felt they would not support his policies towards sexual minorities in the military.

　左翼活動家は特に軍を標的にしています。バラク・オバマ氏が 2009 年 1 月に大統領に就任したとき、彼が最初に行ったことの一つは、将軍や提督から中佐まで、アメリカ軍の将校約 197 人を解雇することでした。その理由は、軍における性的マイノリティに対する彼の政策を、彼らが支持しないだろうと感じたためです。

When I joined the Marine Corps in 1974, Gay people were forbidden from joining the military. At that time, trans gender people hardly existed. Until about 20 years ago, transgenderism was thought of as a mental illness, and it was estimated that 0.03% of the population was transgender.

　私が 1974 年に海兵隊に入隊した当時、ゲイは軍に入隊することが禁じられていました。当時はトランスジェンダーの人々はほとんど存在していませんでした。20 年ほど前までは、トランスジェンダーは精神疾患と考えられており、人口の 0.03 パーセントがトランスジェンダーであると推定されていました。

I have no problem with Gay people in the military. They are completely normal people. However transgenderism is something different. To deny your physical reality, the reality you are born with, does indeed seem to be a type of mental illness. And such people are on medications, which makes their mood swings quite intense. This in my

Chapter 1 Present day America

mind disqualifies them from military service.

　ゲイが軍隊にいても何の問題もありません。彼らは完全に普通の人々です。しかし、トランスジェンダーは別問題です。自分の肉体的な現実、つまり生まれながらに持っている現実を否定することは、確かに一種の精神疾患のように思えます。そして、そのような人々は薬を服用しており、そのせいで気分の変動がかなり激しくなります。これは兵役に就くには不適格だと私は思います。

Another major aspect of the Obama administration has been the introduction of women in combat units. When I was in the Marine Corps in 1975, women could not serve in infantry, artillery, or armor. These were designated as Combat arms.

　オバマ政権のもう一つの大きな特徴は、戦闘部隊への女性の導入です。私が海兵隊にいた 1975 年当時、女性は歩兵、砲兵、機甲部隊に配属できませんでした。これらは戦闘部隊に指定されていました。

The United States Marine Corps has always prided itself on its infantry prowess. Basic training, or "boot camp" was three months when I was in the Marine Corps. Of this period, two weeks were rifle range training, and two weeks infantry school.

　アメリカ海兵隊は、常に歩兵の強さを誇りにしてきました。私が海兵隊にいた頃、基礎訓練、いわゆる「ブートキャンプ」は 3 カ月

でした。このうち2週間はライフル射撃訓練で、2週間は歩兵学校でした。

For those Marines who went on to become professional infantrymen, there was a further 6 month infantry school. After that, they would be assigned to an infantry unit, and after one or two years in the unit, would be considered a professional infantryman.

　プロの歩兵になる海兵隊員は、さらに6カ月間の歩兵学校がありました。その後、歩兵部隊に配属され、部隊に1～2年所属すると、プロの歩兵とみなされます。

As for the 6 month infantry school, some 25% of the troops in the school would fail, and be reassigned to some other job. It was very physically grueling. When President Obama issued the order to integrate women into the infantry, the Marine Corps did a one year study.

　6カ月の歩兵学校については、学校に通う兵士の約25パーセントが不合格となり、他の任務に再配置されます。これは肉体的に非常に過酷なものでした。オバマ大統領が女性を歩兵部隊に組み入れるよう命令を出したとき、海兵隊は1年間の研究を行いました。

They would have all male platoons compete against platoons that were half male and half female. Problems like climbing over a mountain and then carrying out an assault of a mock town. What they found was that all male platoons outdid the mixed platoons in every problem. Also, the

Chapter 1 Present day America

women suffered many more physical injuries than the men.

　男性のみの小隊と、男女半々の小隊を競わせます。山越えや模擬の町を襲撃するといった課題です。すると、男性のみの小隊が男女混合の小隊をどの課題でも上回りました。また、女性は男性よりも多くの身体的損傷を負いました。

Male and female bodies are built differently. Yet this reality is not something that a Leftist can accept. The Army simply created lower physical standards so that women could pass them. For example, men do pushups from their toes, women can do them from their knees.

　男性と女性では身体の構造が異なります。しかし、この現実は左

U.S. Female Soldier and U.S. male Soldier

アメリカ女性兵と男性兵

第1章　現在のアメリカ

翼が受け入れられるものではありません。軍は女性が合格できるように基準を低く設定しました。たとえば、男性はつま先で腕立て伏せをしますが、女性は膝をついて腕立て伏せをします。

The problem is, in combat, there will be no such niceties from a potential enemy. Israel used to have women in front line combat positions, but in the 1973 war it was found that these units tended to surrender quickly in order to spare the women from death.

　問題は、戦場の敵は女性に対してそんな配慮をしてくれないということです。イスラエルはかつて女性を最前線に配置しましたが、1973年の戦争では、女性を死から救うためにこれらの部隊はすぐに降伏する傾向があることが判明しました。

Then there is the problem of sex. This is a very natural human activity. Especially with young people thrown together in an environment that is often dangerous. This especially affects the Navy. The rules are if a female sailor becomes pregnant on a ship, she must be evacuated to a land base in her third month of pregnancy.

　それから、セックスの問題もあります。これは人間としてごく自然な行為です。特に、若い人たちは危険な環境に放り込まれると、なおさらそのような行為が起きやすいです。これは特に海軍に影響を及ぼします。規則では、女性の海軍将兵が洋上で妊娠した場合、妊娠3カ月以内に陸上基地に移さなければなりません。

I have read of at least one incident where an aircraft carrier had to

Chapter 1 Present day America

divert from its mission to fly a female sailor to a land base in Spain. On carriers, it is common for officers to patrol the hanger deck with flashlights at night. The hanger deck on a carrier is quite large, and there are many hidden nooks and crannies where couples can find some privacy to attempt to have sex.

　空母が任務を変更して、女性水兵をスペインの陸上基地に移送しなければならなかったという記事を、一度読んだことがあります。空母では、夜間に士官が懐中電灯を手に格納甲板を巡回するのが一般的です。空母の格納甲板はとても広く、カップルがプライバシーを確保してセックスできる場所がたくさんあります。

In the Army, there are also many problems in this area. In a small unit, friendship between the leaders, the Sergeant, and the men is not encouraged. That is because in combat it is very likely that it is necessary to send a soldier on a dangerous mission. If the other soldiers feel that a certain soldier will not be sent on such a mission because he is a friend of the Sergeant, well unit cohesion begins to disappear. That unit becomes unfit for combat. It is a human characteristic that a woman will use the attractiveness of her sex to gain advantage with male leadership.

　陸軍でも、この領域では多くの問題があります。小規模な部隊では、士官、下士官、兵士の間の友情は奨励されません。戦闘では、兵士を危険な任務に送る必要が生じる可能性が高いためです。ある兵士が下士官と親しいので、そのような任務に送られないだろうと別の兵士が感じた場合、部隊の結束は失われ始めます。その部隊は戦闘に適さなくなります。女性は自分の性的魅力を利用して男性の

指揮官に取り入ることができますが、これは人間の持つ特性です。

The M1 Abrams tank has a crew of four. The most difficult job is the replacement of the tank tread, it often comes off during operations. It takes four people to do this job. Since it is heavy work and difficult, female crew members often refuse to participate.

　M1 エイブラムス戦車の乗員は 4 人です。最も難しい作業は戦車の履帯の交換で、作戦中に履帯が外れてしまうことがよくあります。この作業には 4 人の人員が必要です。力仕事で大変なため、女性乗員は参加を拒否することがよくあります。

With difficulty, three male crew members can do this job. But not two, and that tank will be out of action. The military has one job, that is to protect America from enemy countries. It is not a place to conduct social experiments on the roles between men and women.

　3 人の男性乗員では、この任務をこなすのは困難です。2 人では無理です。そうなると、戦車は機能しなくなります。軍隊の仕事はただ一つ、敵国からアメリカを守ることです。男女の役割分担について社会実験を行う場所ではありません。

I have seen a certain Colonel Wootan of the Air Force on Youtube saying that there are too many White pilots. This Colonel is a White man, but why does he say this? He says White men all think alike, and to achieve more diversity in the military, there needs to fewer White officers.

Chapter 1 Present day America

　Youtube で、空軍のウータン大佐が「白人パイロットが多すぎる」と発言しているのを見たことがあります。この大佐は白人ですが、なぜこんなことを言うのでしょうか。彼は、白人はみんな同じように考えており、軍隊で多様性を高めるには白人将校の数を減らす必要がある、と言っているのです。

This kind of thinking is astounding. I suppose it is what you can expect from country where people believe there are no differences between men and women, and that one can change your biological sex as you like.

　このような考え方には驚かされます。男女の間に違いはなく、生物学的な性別は好きなように変えられると信じている国の人たちからすれば、そのような考えは当然のことなのでしょう。

U.S. Female Soldier

アメリカ女性兵

第1章 現在のアメリカ

Inferior weapons
劣った武器

American weapons have performed dismally in the Ukraine war. Russian weaponry is superior in every way. Well, American weapons are designed to make money for the manufacturers. Russian weapons are designed to defend the country. And the Russians have technical education that is greatly superior to that of Americans.

ウクライナ戦争では、アメリカの兵器は惨憺たる結果しか出ませんでした。ロシアの兵器はあらゆる点で優れています。アメリカの兵器は製造した企業が儲けるために設計されています。ロシアの兵器は国を守るために設計されています。そしてロシア人はアメリカ人よりはるかに優れた技術教育を受けています。

The F-35 fighter jet is a case in point. Development of the F-35 started in 1995, and it has been plagued with problems. It is known as the most expensive weapon system ever. In fact, only about 30% of them are operational. As I write these lines, some 100 F-35 aircraft sit outside the Renton Washington plant, idle. They are awaiting repairs to their malfunctioning computer systems. The computers have a disturbing tendency to crash during flight, and this could cause the aircraft to crash.

F-35戦闘機がその好例です。F-35の開発は1995年に開始されましたが、様々な問題に悩まされてきました。この戦闘機は史上最も高価な兵器システムとして知られています。しかし基本的に、飛行

できるのは30パーセント程度です。この記事を書いている間にも、約100機のF-35がワシントン州レントンの工場の外に放置されています。コンピューターシステムの修理を待っているのです。このコンピューターは飛行中に機能不全(クラッシュ)に陥るという厄介な問題を抱えており、これが航空機の実際の墜落(クラッシュ)を引き起こす可能性があります。

It can only carry four bombs or missiles, this imitation is to preserve the aircraft's stealth. The F-35 has not yet seen any combat. Yet despite these problems, and 400% cost increases, the Pentagon has approved increased production of the F-35, another 1,500 planes.

爆弾またはミサイルは4発しか搭載できませんが、これは航空機のステルス性を維持するためです。F-35による戦闘はまだ一度も行われていません。しかし、これらの問題と400パーセントのコスト増にもかかわらず、国防総省はF-35をさらに1,500機増産することを承認しました。

In 2019, the United States Air Force ordered 80 new F-15 fighter jets, they wanted aircraft that are proven to work.

2019年、アメリカ空軍は80機の新型F-15戦闘機を発注しました。空軍は実用性が実証された航空機を求めていました。

This appears to be an example of military-industrial corruption.

F-35の件は軍事産業の腐敗を示しているようで、ひどいものです。

The M1 Abrams tank has proven inferior in combat. It has virtually no protection against drones, its filters clog on the battlefield, and they must be cleaned two or three times a day, even during battle. The Ukrainian troops don't like them.

　M1エイブラムス戦車は戦闘では劣っていることが証明されています。ドローンに対する防御力は事実上なく、戦場でフィルターが詰まるし、戦闘の最中であっても1日に2、3回掃除しなくてはなりません。ウクライナ軍はこれを嫌っています。

America has totally failed at producing a hypersonic missile, while Russia has been operating its Kinzhal hypersonic missile for well over a year.

　アメリカは極超音速ミサイルの開発に完全に失敗していますが、ロシアはキンジャール極超音速ミサイルを1年以上にわたって運用しています。

Next year, America retires 19 warships, while only building 6 new ships. This is because of leftist policies that do not emphasize technical education. America simply does not have enough trained technical workers.

　来年、アメリカは19隻の軍艦を退役させる一方で、新しく建造されるのは6隻のみです。これは、技術訓練を重視しない左派の政策の影響です。アメリカでは熟練した技術者が不足しています。

On the other hand, Russia possesses excellent weapons, like the Su-57 fighter. Russian air defense systems like the S-400 and the S-500 are the best in the world. Russia also excels in tanks and artillery. The difference is that Russian society has none of the progressive thinking about diversity, but instead praises actual ability. Americans on the other hand are always boasting about great they are, when the reality is they are not really very good at anything.

一方、ロシアはSu-57戦闘機のような優れた兵器を保有しています。S-400やS-500などのロシアの防空システムは世界最高です。ロシアは戦車や大砲でも優れています。アメリカと違うのは、ロシア社会には多様性に関する進歩的な考えがまったくなく、実際の能力を評価する点です。一方、アメリカ人はいつも自分たちは優れていると自慢しますが、実際にはそれほど優秀ではありません。

Can America really defend Japan? The answer is no, they cannot defend themselves. Japanese people should wake up, not simply believing what Americans claim, and study the facts.

アメリカは本当に日本を守れますか？　答えはノーです。アメリカは自国を守ることもできません。日本人は目を覚まし、アメリカ人の言うことを鵜呑みにせず、事実を学ぶべきです。

The militia movement
民兵運動

Japanese people are quite aware that basically, although rules vary by state, Americans may legally possess guns. They are less aware of the existence of the militia movement.

　日本人は、州によってルールは異なるものの、アメリカ人が銃を所持することは基本的に合法であるということはよく知っています。しかし、民兵運動の存在についてはあまり知りません。

This is an organized movement of gun owners, who organize themselves along military style lines. They train and organize to protect themselves from the United States Federal government.

　これは、軍隊の様式に沿って武装した銃所有者の組織的な運動です。彼らは、合衆国連邦政府から自分たちを守るために訓練し、組織を作っています。

They are not controlled in any way by the United States government. In fact, they regard the federal Government as an enemy. They are conservative, and tend to believe in Christian Fundamentalism. They also tend to be Trump supporters.

　彼らはアメリカ政府からいかなる形でも管理されていません。実際、彼らは連邦政府を敵とみなしています。彼らは保守的で、キリスト教原理主義を信じる傾向があります。また、彼らはトランプを支持する傾向が見られます。

They often conduct military training on weekends. There are approximately 300 groups across America. The size of these groups range from a few hundred people to around 30,000 for the largest. I

Chapter 1 Present day America

believe there is a total of at least 300,000 members.

　彼らは週末に軍事訓練を行うことが多いです。アメリカ全土に300ほどのグループがあります。グループの規模は数百人から、最大で約3万人。メンバーの総数は少なくとも30万人いると思います。

Although they don't have unified leadership, they do have religion as a unifying factor, and this could make them quite capable of becoming a National force in a civil war.

　統一されたリーダーシップはないものの、宗教という共通の要素があります。そしてそれによって、彼らは内戦における国民的勢力となる可能性があります。

From December 2019 to January 2020, Democrats gained control of the Virginia State legislature and governorship. The Left then attempted to restrict gun ownership in Virginia. I believe this was a test case before a total takeover of America by the radical Left.

　2019年12月から2020年1月にかけて、民主党はバージニア州議会と州知事の権力を獲得しました。その後、左派はバージニア州での銃の所有を制限しようとしました。これは、アメリカが急進左派に完全に支配される前に起きるであろう兆候だと私は考えています。

The attempt failed completely. The State National Guard outright refused orders to investigate gun owners. Militia members mobilized, and it became clear that violence would result if any controls or restrictions on gun ownership was enacted in Virginia.

　この試みは完全に失敗に終わりました。州兵は銃所有者を調査せよという命令をきっぱりと拒否しました。民兵が動員され、バージニア州で銃の所有に対する規制や制限が実施されれば武装蜂起に発展することが明らかとなりました。

This was a great victory for the Right, and Democrats now are in terror of the armed Right and a Trump victory in November.

　これは右派にとって大きな勝利であり、民主党は今や武装した右派と11月のトランプ勝利を恐れています。

The Migrants
移民たち

Under the Biden administration, some ten million migrants have arrived in the United States, during the last three and half years. If Donald Trump becomes President in January, it is likely that he will attempt to remove them, and that military force will be used.

　バイデン政権下では、過去3年半の間に約1000万人の不法移民がアメリカに入国しました。ドナルド・トランプ氏が1月に大統領に就任すれば、移民の排除を試み、軍事力も行使される可能性が高いです。

Chapter 1 Present day America

These illegal gangs have shown some ability to combine with domestic Latin Americans to abet their criminal activities. If an American government attempts to forcibly expel them, this could evolve into a guerrilla type conflict in urban areas.

　入国した違法ギャングは、国内のラテン系アメリカ人と結託して犯罪行為を助長する傾向も見られます。アメリカ政府が彼らを強制的に追放しようとすれば、都市部でのゲリラ的な紛争に発展する可能性があります。

Trump border wall

トランプ国境の壁

The Christian Fundamentalists
キリスト教原理主義者（福音派）

Many Japanese people have gradually become aware of the Christian Fundamentalist movement. What are they? Well, basically they take a strict interpretation of the Bible. They believe every word in the Bible is the true word of God, and must be obeyed.

　多くの日本人が徐々にキリスト教原理主義運動に気付くようになりました。キリスト教原理主義運動とは何でしょうか？　基本的に彼らは聖書を厳密に解釈します。聖書の言葉はすべて神の真の言葉であり、従わなければならないと信じています。

They do not believe other groups, such as Lutherans, Methodists, Catholics are true Christians. They are concentrated in Pentecostal and Baptist sects. They believe that to become a true Christian, one must be born again, or baptized again, into their church.

　彼らは、ルーテル派、メソジスト派、カトリックなどの他のグループが真のキリスト教徒であるとは信じていません。彼らはペンテコステ派とバプテスト派に集中しています。彼らは、真のキリスト教徒になるには、彼らの教会で新生しなければならない、すなわち再び洗礼を受けなければならないと信じています。

They believe that to save America they must control society.

Chapter 1 Present day America

　彼らはアメリカを救うには社会をコントロールしなければならないと信じています。

They have a philosophy to do this, it is called the "Seven Mountains". These are Family, Religion, Education, Media, Entertainment, Business, and Government. They believe that for America to become a decent nation, they must lead and dominate in these areas.

　彼らにはこれを実行するための哲学があり、それは「七つの山」と呼ばれています。家族、宗教、教育、メディア、娯楽、ビジネス、そして政府です。アメリカがまともな国になるためには、これらの分野で主導権を握り、支配しなければならないと彼らは信じています。

In practical terms, what this means is that only Christian Fundamentalist can be school teachers, appear on television, become a company president, or a politician. It also means that followers of other groups such as Christians, Moslems and Buddhists will not be able to vote in elections. These people will become second class citizens.

　つまり、これはキリスト教原理主義者だけが学校の先生、テレビ出演者、会社の社長、政治家になれることを意味します。また、キリスト教徒、イスラム教徒、仏教徒など他のグループの信者は選挙で投票できないことも意味します。これらの人々は二級市民になります。

In particular, they are very anti LGBT. They will exterminate LGBT people. These people will be offered a chance to convert to heterosexuality. If they do not, they will be executed. I suspect such execution will be carried out as public spectacles in towns across America.

　特に彼らはLGBTに対して強い反感を持っています。彼らはLGBTの人々を根絶しようとするでしょう。これらの人々には異性愛に改宗する機会が与えられます。もし改宗しなければ、彼らは処刑されます。私は、アメリカ中の町で見せしめとして公開処刑が行われるのではないかと考えています。

They are very against biology, especially Darwin's theory of evolution. They believe that the earth was created 6,000 years ago and that humans interacted with dinosaurs. All science education and application in America will be required to follow their Biblical ideas. Naturally, this will be a disaster, and America will cease to be a technological society.

　彼らは生物学、特にダーウィンの進化論に非常に反発しています。彼らは地球が6000年前に創造され、人間が共存と交流していたと信じています。アメリカにおけるすべての科学教育と科学の実用は、彼らの聖書の考えに従うことが求められます。当然、これは悲惨な結果をもたらし、アメリカはテクノロジーの社会ではなくなるでしょう。

This is not in the Bible, but was made by calculations by an Irish Bishop in the year 1,000

こういう話は聖書には書かれていませんが、西暦1000年にアイルランドの司教が算出したものです。

In their own schools, and they have them, they teach Creation theory, which follows the Bible. They teach, for example, that humans and dinosaurs coexisted, until dinosaurs became corrupted by sin, and some became meat eaters.

彼らの学校では聖書に基づいた創造論が教えられており、例えば、人間と恐竜は共存していたが、恐竜が罪を犯して堕落し、一部が肉食動物になったと教えているのです。

These Christian Fundamentalists dominate in rural America. Some 25% of Americans are hard core believers, another 25% are less hardcore. They all form former President Trump's power base. In fact, he had around three such people in his cabinet.

これらのキリスト教原理主義者は、アメリカの農村部で優勢です。アメリカ人の約25パーセントは熱心な信者で、25パーセントはそれほど熱心ではありません。彼らはすべて、トランプ前大統領の支持基盤を形成しています。実際、彼の閣僚にはそのような人物が3人ほどいました。

If they come to dominate America again, it will be very difficult for Japan to deal with these people. They will approach every problem, every relationship, from a literal belief in the Bible.

もし彼らが再びアメリカを支配するようになれば、日本が彼らに対処するのは非常に困難となるでしょう。彼らはあらゆる問題、あらゆる人間関係で、聖書を文字通り信じるという信念に基づいて取り組むでしょう。

Since Christian Fundamentalists believe every part of the Bible is actual truth, they also believe in the story of Armageddon, and the return of Jesus. That is these people are fervent supporters of Israel.

キリスト教原理主義者は聖書の記述はすべて真実であると信じているので、ハルマゲドンの物語やイエスの再臨も信じています。つまり、これらの人々はイスラエルの熱烈な支持者なのです。

Basically, they believe this would involve world wide nuclear war, in which most inhabitants of the earth will perish. But they do not care. They believe that since they worship God correctly, they will be brought to Heaven. In fact, a large number of them will welcome such an event.

彼らは基本的に、それが世界規模の核戦争を引き起こし、地球上のほとんどの住民が死滅するだろうと信じています。しかし、彼らはそんなことは気にしません。彼らは、神への信仰が正しいのだから、天国に導かれると信じています。実際、彼らの中の多くの人々が、そのような出来事を歓迎するでしょう。

Japanese people will have a difficult time understanding this, but it is true. Well, 25% of Americans believe the earth is flat. Frankly,

Americans are not known for being an intellectual people.

　日本人には理解しにくいでしょうが、これは事実です。アメリカ人の 25 パーセントは地球は平らだと信じています。はっきり言うと、アメリカ人は知的な国民だとは評価されていません。

The Ukraine war, an enormous military and foreign policy disaster
ウクライナ戦争

The Ukraine war is turning out to be America's greatest military defeat. It is a totally self-inflicted disaster caused by hubris and conceit. American education is famous for "dumbing down", or simplifying complex subjects. Thus, Americans have no true understanding of history. When the American government sponsored the Maidan revolution in Ukraine in 2014, they had little or no knowledge about Russia, or Russian history.

　ウクライナ戦争はアメリカにとって最大の軍事的敗北となりつつあります。これは傲慢さと自惚れが招いた完全に自業自得の惨事です。アメリカの教育は複雑な問題を「単純化」することで有名です。そのため、アメリカ人は歴史を正しく理解していません。アメリカ政府が 2014 年にウクライナのマイダン革命を支援したとき、彼らはロシアやロシアの歴史についてほとんど何も知りませんでした。

Phrases such as "A gas station masquerading as a country" were repeated throughout the US government. What this means is that Americans thought that Russia might have oil resources, it was not a viable state. The Americans simply had no idea that their plans had no chance for success.

「国家を名乗るガソリンスタンド」といった言葉が、アメリカ政府内で繰り返し語られました。これは、アメリカ人がロシアには石油資源があるかもしれないが、生き残れる国ではないと考えていたことを意味します。アメリカ人は、自分たちの計画が成功する見込みがないことに全く気づいていなかったのです。

They believed that by training the Ukrainian army, and building it up, they could inflict a military defeat upon Russia. Both Napoleon and Hitler thought they could beat Russian forces when they first began their offensives against Russia.

彼らは、ウクライナ軍を訓練し、増強することで、ロシアに軍事的敗北をもたらすことができると信じていました。ナポレオンもヒトラーも、ロシアに対する攻撃を開始した当初は、ロシアに勝てると考えていました。

But the Ukrainian forces have only once showed military domination over Russian forces. In the initial stage of the war, Russia sent an armored column in the direction of Kiev. The Ukrainian government requested its withdrawal, saying it could not negotiate with Russian troops so close to Kiev.

しかし、ウクライナ軍がロシア軍に対して軍事的優位性を示したのは一度だけです。戦争の初期段階では、ロシアはキエフ方面に機甲部

Chapter 1 Present day America

隊を投入しました。ウクライナ政府は、キエフにこれほど近いロシア軍と交渉することはできないとして、その撤退を要求しました。

Well, Russia withdrew its troops, and Kiev claimed a military victory, even though there had been no fighting. Later on, Russia withdrew troops that had crossed the Dnieper at Kherson. The retreat was voluntary, and conducted without interference by the Ukrainian forces. Again, the Ukrainian government claimed this as a military victory.

　ロシアは軍隊を撤退させ、キエフでは戦闘がなかったにもかかわらず、ウクライナは軍事的勝利を主張しました。その後、ロシアはヘルソンでドニエプル川を渡った部隊を撤退させました。撤退は自発的なもので、ウクライナ軍の干渉なしに行われました。ウクライナ政府は再びこれを軍事的勝利だと主張しました。

Ukraine did make a counter attack in the Kharkov area, where only one Russian battalion, about 600 men, was holding the front. They advanced with some 30,000 men. One Russian border company, a few hundred men completely stalled the advance. The Russians managed to withdraw in good order, and with few losses.

　ウクライナはハリコフ地域で反撃しましたが、そこではロシア軍の1個大隊（約600名）が前線を守っていただけでした。ウクライナ軍は約3万人の兵力をもって進撃しました。ロシア軍の国境部隊（数百名）がウクライナ軍の進撃を完全に阻止しました。ロシア軍は秩序を保ち、損失を最小限に抑えて撤退に成功しました。

However, the Ukrainian force lost one third of its numbers due to Russian artillery and air strikes. Even though the Ukrainian forces advanced over ground, do to their severe losses, this cannot be called a victory.

　しかし、ウクライナ軍はロシア軍の砲撃と空爆により兵力の3分の1を失いました。ウクライナ軍は前進したものの、甚大な損失を被ったため、これを勝利と呼ぶことはできません。

Very quickly in the war, the Ukrainian air force has been destroyed. Russia has always maintained artillery superiority, Throughout the war the Russians have fired some 20,000 shells a day compared to Ukraine firing 6,000 a day. In early 2024, the Ukrainian rate dropped to 1,000. The reason is NATO stocks of artillery shells have been exhausted, in both Europe and the US.

　戦争開始後、ウクライナ空軍はあっという間に壊滅しました。ロシアは常に砲兵の優位を保っており、戦争中ロシアは1日あたり約2万発の砲弾を消費したのに対し、ウクライナは1日あたり6000発でした。2024年初頭、ウクライナの砲弾消費数は1000発にまで減少しました。その理由は、NATOの砲弾の備蓄がヨーロッパとアメリカの両方で枯渇したためです。

The Russians have been able to increase production of artillery shells, missiles, tanks and all sorts of military equipment. America has been able to somewhat increase artillery shells, but they are greatly hampered by a lack of engineers. The effects of decades of Left-wing educational policies in destroying education are beginning to show.

Chapter 1 Present day America

ロシアは砲弾、ミサイル、戦車、その他あらゆる軍需品の生産を増やすことができました。アメリカは砲弾を多少増産できましたが、技術者の不足によって大きく妨げられています。左翼教育政策が教育を破壊してきた数十年の影響が現れ始めています。

Casualties have been 10 to 1. For every Russian soldier that died in the war, 10 Ukrainians have died. In the summer of 2023, the Western powers pressured Ukraine to make an offensive towards the Sea of Azov coast. Russia had three lines of heavy fortifications. Russia also had a great superiority in artillery, and total air superiority. It was a disaster, the Ukrainian forces were decimated. They only advanced a few kilometers.

戦死者の比率は 10 対 1 です。戦争で亡くなったロシア兵 1 人につき、ウクライナ兵 10 人が亡くなりました。2023 年の夏、西側諸国はウクライナに圧力をかけ、アゾフ海沿岸への攻撃を命じました。ロシアは三重の防衛線を築いていました。ロシアはまた、砲兵力でも圧倒的な優位性があり、航空戦でも完全な優位性を持っていました。この攻撃は悲惨な結果を招き、ウクライナ軍は壊滅的打撃を受けました。前進できたのはわずか数キロでした。

The Americans in particular, and other Western powers believed that Russian forces were weak due to heavy losses. That was completely untrue. It was complete fantasy among American and European leaders. And for that fantasy, many Ukrainian men died.

特にアメリカや他の西側諸国は、ロシア軍が大きな損失を被った

第1章　現在のアメリカ

ため弱体化したと考えていました。しかし、それは全くの誤りでした。アメリカやヨーロッパの指導者たちの完全な幻想でした。そして、その幻想のために多くのウクライナ人が亡くなりました。

The Ukrainians have never been able to dominate on the battlefield, only perhaps once in their Kharkov offensive. Always, it is Ukraine reacting to Russian moves. The result is that Ukraine suffers extreme casualties in defending some town which is eventually lost to the Russians.

　ウクライナ軍は戦場で優位に立つことができず、優位に立てたのはハリコフ攻勢のときだけでした。いつもウクライナはロシア軍の動きに反応して後手に回っています。その結果、ウクライナは町を守るために多大な犠牲を払い、最終的にはその町をロシア軍に奪われることになります。

Ukraine should try to use a more mobile defense, but that is impossible due to the total loss of the Ukrainian Air Force. The West has long talked about supplying F-16 fighter jets to Ukraine to rebuild their Air Force.

　ウクライナはより機動性の高い防衛手段を講じるべきですが、ウクライナ空軍が完全に失われたためそれは不可能です。西側諸国は長い間、ウクライナ空軍の再建のためF-16戦闘機を供与することを検討してきました。

But the F-16 is 50 years old. Present day Russian fighter aircraft like the Su-57 are much more advanced. And Russian Air Defense has proven to be incredible. The S 400 and S 500 Air Defense weapons are the best in the world.

しかし、F-16 は 50 年前の機体です。現在のロシアの戦闘機、Su-57 などははるかに先進的です。そしてロシアの防空能力は驚異的であることが証明されています。ロシアの地対空ミサイルシステム S400、S500 は世界最高です。

In any case America has only been able to train 6 pilots. For them to even take to the air in an F-16 over Ukraine would be a suicide mission.

それに、アメリカは6人のウクライナ軍パイロットしか訓練できていません。彼らが F-16 でウクライナ上空を飛行することさえ、自殺行為となるでしょう。

The American Patriot missile system just does not compare. Well, many years ago, I had a friend who was a former Vice President of Boeing. He once laughingly told me that "The Patriot missile does not work !".

ロシアの対空ミサイルは、アメリカのパトリオットミサイルシステムとは比べものになりません。何年か前、ボーイング社の元副社長だった友人が、笑いながら私にこう言いました。「パトリオットミサイルなんか役に立たないよ！」

And why does not the US supply Ukraine with advanced F-35 fighter jets? Well, they don't work either. Right now, over 100 F-35 aircraft are parked outside the Lockheed factory. They are undergoing repairs to the computer software.

　では、なぜアメリカはウクライナに最新鋭のF-35戦闘機を供与しないのでしょうか？　実はそれも機能しないからです。現在、100機以上のF-35がロッキード社の工場の外に駐機しています。F-35はソフトウェアの修正作業が行われています。

It seems that they must be rebooted in flight. The reason 100 aircraft are parked outside the factory is that the military refuses to take them. They are that deficient.

　飛行中に再起動する必要があるようです。工場の外に100機駐機したままなのは、軍が引き取りを拒否しているためです。それほど欠陥があるのです。

The Ukrainians are very unhappy with the American M1 Abrams tank. In combat, its engine filters need to be changed several times a day. It is virtually defenseless against drone attacks.

　ウクライナ人はアメリカのM1エイブラムス戦車に非常に不満を抱いています。戦闘中、そのエンジンフィルターは1日に何度も交換する必要があります。ドローン攻撃に対しては事実上無防備です。

As Russia has basic drone superiority across the front, they prioritize attacks against the M1 Abrams.

Chapter 1 Present day America

　ロシアは前線全体でドローンの優位性を確立しているため、M1エイブラムスを優先的に攻撃しています。

For Japan, as dependent on American weapons as we are, this is a disaster. But for the Americans, the plane is a success, since it is expensive and makes money for Lockheed stock holders.

　アメリカの兵器に依存している日本にとって、これは大変な問題です。しかし、アメリカにとって、この飛行機は成功です。高価な機体であり、ロッキード社の株主に利益をもたらすからです。

In fact, all American and NATO weapon systems deployed to Ukraine have proven to be inferior to Russian systems. Perhaps Japan should buy weapons from Russia? Actually, this is a crisis for Japan, the best solution is to develop our own weapons.

　実際、ウクライナに配備されたアメリカとNATOの兵器システムはすべて、ロシアのシステムより劣っていることが証明されています。日本はロシアから兵器を購入した方がよいのでしょうか？実際のところ、日本にとって危機的状況であり、最善の解決策は独自の兵器を開発することです。

And the Ukrainians advertised their offensive in the media. Incredibly amateurish. In fact all throughout the war, President Zelensky of Ukraine has shown a preference for terrorist like operations, and public relations type operations, for example, attacks against the Kerch bridge, or against the Zaporozhye nuclear power plant, which is behind

Russian lines.

　ウクライナ軍は、メディアで自軍の攻勢を宣伝しました。信じられないほど素人同然のやり方です。実際、戦争中ずっと、ウクライナのゼレンスキー大統領は、例えばケルチ橋やロシア軍の後方に位置するザポリージャ原子力発電所への攻撃など、テロのような作戦や広報目的の作戦を好んで行っています。

Even if the Ukrainians some how managed to destroy the Kerch bridge, it would have no effect on Russian operations in Crimea. There are many ferries and ports. Also, the Russian have fought along the coast of the sea of Azov, and established a land corridor into the Crimea.

　たとえウクライナ軍がケルチ橋を破壊できたとしても、クリミア半島におけるロシア軍の作戦には影響がありません。フェリーや港がたくさんあります。また、ロシア軍はアゾフ海沿岸で戦闘を行い、クリミア半島への陸路を確保しています。

And throughout the war while Ukrainian troops were suffering from a lack of artillery support, Ukraine would shell civilian areas in Donetsk and Lugansk. In February of 2024 the Ukrainians killed some 28 civilians in a bakery in the town of Lisichansk, in Lugansk.

　そして戦争中ずっと、ウクライナ軍が砲兵の支援不足に苦しんでいた間、ウクライナはドネツクとルガンスクの民間地域を砲撃し続けました。2024年2月、ウクライナ軍はルガンスクのリシチャン

Chapter 1 Present day America

スク町のパン屋で約 28 人の民間人を殺害しました。

These attacks have no effect whatsoever on Ukrainian military operations, They only show the nastiness of the Ukrainian government. Well, even before the war started, the Ukrainians who ran the country were pretty nasty. I remember seeing pictures of Ukrainians being taped to telephone poles, both men and women. They had had their pants pulled down to their ankles, and were left half nude in public display. Why? They had been heard to speak the Russian language.

　これらの攻撃はウクライナ軍の作戦にはまったく関係がなく、ウクライナ政府の非道を示すだけです。戦争が始まる前から、実際に国を動かしていたウクライナ人はかなり悪質でした。ウクライナ人が男性も女性も電柱にテープで固定されている写真を見たことがあります。彼らはズボンを足首まで引きずり下ろされ、公衆の面前で半裸にされていました。なぜでしょう？　彼らがロシア語を話しているのが聞こえたからです。

The truth is, half of the Ukraine of the 2014 borders speaks Russian as their native language. Even President Zelensky does not really speak Ukrainian.

　実のところ、2014 年の国境に接するウクライナの住民の半数はロシア語を母国語としています。ゼレンスキー大統領ですらウクライナ語を十分に話せるわけではありません。

第1章　現在のアメリカ

The Ukrainian endgame
ウクライナ戦争の今後

Now, in the summer of 2024, the Ukrainian army is beginning to break. They do not fight hard to defend positions. They make unauthorized retreats. Surrenders have greatly increased.

　2024年夏の今、ウクライナ軍は崩壊し始めています。彼らは陣地を守るために激しく戦いません。彼らは許可なく撤退しています。降伏が大幅に増加しています。

The F-16 fighters have finally arrived, but there are only six pilots. and the planes are old. The whole effort is some kind of bad joke.

　F-16戦闘機がようやく到着しましたが、パイロットはたった6人しかいません。しかも飛行機は古いです。この取り組みは、一種の悪い冗談です。

European countries are cutting their aid, They know Ukraine is finished. Germany is halving is contribution to Ukraine next year. Yet Japanese Prime Minister Kishida wishes to continue to support Ukraine. He is throwing good money after bad.

　ヨーロッパ諸国は援助を削減しています。彼らはウクライナが終わったことを知っています。ドイツは来年ウクライナへの援助を半減させます。しかし、日本の岸田首相はウクライナへの支援を継続したいと望んでいます。彼は無駄なお金をつぎ込んでいます。

Chapter 1 Present day America

It seems that America is only concerned with Ukraine surviving until next year, so that they can blame the collapse on a possible Trump administration. Personally, I don't think Ukraine can survive that long.

　アメリカは、来年までウクライナが存続できるかどうかだけに関心があるようです。それまで存続できれば、崩壊の原因をトランプ政権のせいにできるからです。個人的には、ウクライナがそこまで長く存続できるとは思えません。

A new American military leadership has been appointed for Japan and South Korea. While South Korea can send troops overseas, Japan has constitutional restrictions. And America totally lacks ammunition, and the ability to produce it. America will lose any war it starts, especially with China.

　日本と韓国に新しいアメリカの軍事指導者が任命されました。韓国は海外に軍隊を派遣できますが、日本には憲法上の制約があります。そしてアメリカは、弾薬も、それを生産する能力もまったく不足しています。アメリカは戦争を仕掛ければ必ず負けるでしょう。特に相手が中国なら。

America is a failing state, and desperate to prove it can still win a war. Japan should be careful not to be drawn into this. America has no leadership. It has become obvious to the world that the President is a Zombie, so America drifts into disaster. Japanese leadership should wake up, and not bring Japan into that same disaster.

　アメリカはすでに破綻国家であり、戦争に勝てることを示そうと

必死です。日本はそれに巻き込まれないよう注意すべきです。アメリカには統率力がありません。大統領がゾンビであることは世界中に明らかになっており、アメリカは破滅へと向かっています。日本のリーダーは目を覚ますべきであり、日本を同じ破滅へと導いてはなりません。

The Middle Eastern conflict
中東戦争

The Biden administration is also facing a serious challenge in the Israel and Hamas war. Despite killing tens of thousands of Palestine civilians, Israel has not been able to dominate Gaza.

　バイデン政権はイスラエルとハマスの戦争でも深刻な問題に直面しています。イスラエルは数万人のパレスチナ民間人を殺害したにもかかわらず、ガザを制圧できていません。

Now there is talk of a further attack into Lebanon against Hezbollah. Israel has failed here before while Hezbollah has grown stronger. This conflict is doing serious damage to President Biden's reelection chances.

　現在、さらにレバノンのヒズボラに対して攻撃が行われるのではないかと噂されています。イスラエルは以前ここで失敗しており、その後ヒズボラは勢力を強めています。この紛争はバイデン大統領の再選に深刻なダメージを与えています。

Another great mistake of the Biden administration is the destruction of the oil dollar. I remember when President Biden first traveled to Saudi Arabia on a state visit. He was accompanied by Secretary of State Blinken. Upon their return to America, Secretary of State Blinken boasted about he pressured Saudi Arabia's ruler Mohammed bin Salman about LGBT rights.

　バイデン政権のもう一つの大きな失策は、ペトロダラー（ドル建て原油取引）の破壊です。バイデン大統領が初めてサウジアラビアを公式訪問したときのことを覚えています。彼にはブリンケン国務長官が同行していました。帰国後、ブリンケン国務長官はLGBTの権利保護についてサウジアラビアの君主ムハンマド・ビン・サルマンに積極的に働きかけたと自慢しました。

Saudi Arabia is a country where homosexual activity is punished by execution. They certainly would not want to hear such a lecture by Secretary of State Anthony Blinken. It was not long after that that Saudi Arabia began selling oil in Russian rubles and Chinese yuan. This has greatly damaged the United States.

　サウジアラビアは同性愛行為が死刑になる国です。彼らは、そのようなブリンケン国務長官の御高説は賜りたくなかったでしょう。それから間もなく、サウジアラビアはロシア・ルーブルと中国元で石油を売り始めました。これはアメリカに大きな打撃を与えました。

On June 9th 2024 Saudi Arabia did not extend the agreement with the United States concerning the petro dollar. This will do tremendous damage to the standing of the United States in the world.

　2024年6月9日、サウジアラビアはペトロダラーに関するアメリカとの協定を延長しませんでした。これはアメリカの世界における地位に甚大なダメージを与えることになるでしょう。

The bane of America, "Feminism"
諸悪の元凶「フェミニスト」

The American Biden administration has made another great error in driving Russia and China into a deep alliance with each other. Between 2008 and 2014, Russia was war gaming a war with China. They are not natural allies.

　アメリカのバイデン政権は、ロシアと中国を深い同盟関係に追い込むという、さらに大きな誤りを犯しました。2008年から2014年の間、ロシアは中国との戦争を想定していました。両国は本来、同盟国ではありません。

Yet American ineptitude of the Biden administration has pushed them together, in a strong alliance. And this has led to the creation of the BRICS movement, which is an alternative power bloc to America. It seems that the Biden administration is trying to commit national suicide.

　しかし、無能なバイデン政権が、彼らを強力な同盟関係へと押しやりました。そして、これがアメリカに代わる勢力圏である

Chapter 1 Present day America

BRICSの創設につながりました。バイデン政権はアメリカの自死を図ろうとしているようです。

A serious question can be asked, why are Americans so incompetent? Well this question has one answer, Feminists. American women as a rule, are tremendous egoists. When I was young and lived in America, America culture always emphasized respecting women.

　アメリカ人はなぜこんなに無能なのか、という素朴な疑問が湧くかもしれません。この疑問に対する答えは一つ、フェミニストです。アメリカ人女性は総じて、とてつもないエゴイストです。私がアメリカに住んでいた若い頃、アメリカ文化は常に女性を尊重することを強調していました。

You were supposed to be polite to women, and show them deference. From this cultural custom, American women, in the time since WWII, developed an extreme sense of entitlement. They feel that they don't have enough respect, and that they have been repressed and abused by American society.

　女性に対しては礼儀正しく、敬意を払うことが求められていました。この文化的慣習により、第二次世界大戦以降、アメリカの女性は過度の権利意識を持つようになりました。彼女たちは、十分な敬意を払われていないと感じ、アメリカ社会から抑圧され、虐待されてきたと感じています。

So the elite women of American society decided they must destroy

America. They began with education. American women totally dominate American education. They gradually eliminated traditional Western cultural education in history and literature. For example, very few universities teach Shakespeare anymore. It is much more fashionable to teach about minority authors, born in non English speaking countries.

　そこでアメリカ社会のエリート女性たちは、アメリカを破壊しなければならないと決意したのです。彼女たちはまず教育から始めました。アメリカの教育は完全にアメリカ人女性によって支配されています。そして、歴史や文学における西洋の伝統的な文化教育を徐々に排除していきました。例えば、シェイクスピアを教える大学はもうほとんどありません。今は、英語圏以外の国で生まれたマイノリティの作家を教えるほうが一般的になっています。

But to American women, such basic culture must be destroyed. Also history education has been destroyed by American women. Now we have history that strongly emphasizes the role of the Black minority in American history.

　アメリカの女性にとって、そのような基本的な文化は破壊されなければならないのです。歴史教育もアメリカ人女性によって破壊されてきました。現在、アメリカの歴史において黒人マイノリティの役割を強く強調した歴史が教えられています。

An example of this is the New York Times sponsored 1619 project. It teaches that American history began when the first Black slaves landed

Chapter 1 Present day America

in America. The truth is that while Black slaves did play an important role in American history, they did not play a Central role.

　その一例が、ニューヨークタイムズが後援する1619プロジェクトです。このプロジェクトでは、アメリカの歴史は最初の黒人奴隷がアメリカに上陸したときに始まったと教えています。しかし実際は、黒人奴隷はアメリカの歴史において重要な役割を果たしましたが、中心的な役割を果たしたわけではありません。

That Central role was played by White, Anglo Saxon immigrants. American women hate this truth. So they try to destroy it. For the average Japanese person reading this book, they may find this truth paradoxical.

　その中心的な役割を担ったのは、白人のアングロサクソン系移民です。アメリカ人女性はこの真実を嫌っています。だから、この事実を覆そうとします。この本を読んでいる一般的な日本人には、これは不可解に思えるかもしれません。

But it is true. American women hate, and are jealous about strong White men. They hated their fathers for giving them rules to live by when they were children. That is why they have always been in revolt against traditional American society, and have tried to destroy it. Actually, they have greatly succeeded in their quest to destroy America.

　しかし、これは紛れもない事実です。アメリカの女性は強い白人男性を憎み、嫉妬しています。彼女たちは、子供の頃に生きるため

のルールを課した父親を憎みました。だからこそ、彼女たちは常に伝統的なアメリカ社会に反抗し、それを破壊しようとしてきたのです。実際、彼女たちはアメリカを破壊するという試みにおいて大成功を収めてきました。

The Feminist destruction of the Education system
フェミニストによる教育破壊

For some time, people were not alarmed by the Feminist destruction of Liberal Arts education. But eventually the Feminists expanded their destruction of education to STEM topics. That is Science, Technology, Engineering, and Math.

しばらくの間、人々はフェミニストによる文系教育の破壊を問題視していませんでした。しかし、やがてフェミニストは教育の破壊を理系の分野、科学、技術、工学、数学にまで手を伸ばしました。

When I was in high school in America, someone who was going into a technical field would have one year of Algebra, one year of Geometry, one year of Trigonometry, and one year of Calculus. Now those four years are cut down into two years. Cuts in Physics, Biology, and Chemistry are similar.

私がアメリカの高校生だった頃、技術系の学科に進む人は代数学を1年、幾何学を1年、三角法を1年、微積分を1年履修していました。今では、その4科目は合計2年に短縮されています。物理学、

Chapter 1 Present day America

生物学、化学も同様です。

The Feminists celebrated this, saying they were disposing of education by "Old White Men". Unfortunately, it is "Old White Men" who created America, so erasing their contributions is not a good idea.

　フェミニストたちはこれを祝福し、「過去の白人男性」による教育を廃止したと主張しました。しかし残念ながら、その「過去の白人男性」こそがアメリカを作り上げたのであり、彼らの功績を消し去るのは賢明な考えではありません。

What Americans do teach, in fact greatly promote, is LGBT. American schools and medical institutions like hospitals have been completely taken over by pharmaceutical companies and radical Leftists.

　アメリカ人が教えていること、そして実際に大いに推進しているのはLGBTです。アメリカの学校や病院などの医療機関は、製薬会社と過激な左翼主義者に完全に乗っ取られています。

In school, at all levels, students are indoctrinated that they are not the sex they were born with. The teachers say that this sex is not immutable, that the doctor arbitrarily assigned them a sex at birth. Their true sex is what they feel it is. The social media Facebook for example has 53 some different types of sex to select your own identity from.

　学校では、どの段階でも、生徒たちは自分が生まれたときに決められた性別とは異なる可能性があると教え込まれます。教師たち

は、この性別は不変のものではなく、医者が生まれたときに恣意的に割り当てたものだと言います。彼らのいう本当の性別とは、彼らがそう感じているものです。たとえば、ソーシャルメディアのFacebookには、自分のアイデンティティを選択するための53種類の性別が用意されています。

The schools, teachers and administrators, who are mostly radical Leftists, encourage the children to change sexual identity. If the parents at home resist this, the school will help the child to keep a secret at school. A child leaves home dressed as a boy, named John.

　学校、教師、管理職の多くは過激な左翼で、子供たちに性自認を変えることを奨励しています。親がこれに抵抗した場合、学校は子供が家庭で秘密を保てるよう手助けします。ジョンという名の子供が男の子の格好をして家を出ます。

At school, there is a changing room where the child can change into girls clothing, and adopt a different name, say Betsy. Cross sex hormones, for example estrogen for boys, and testosterone for girls, can be administered in most Left-wing states from the age of 8 years old.

　学校には更衣室があり、そこで子供は女の子の服に着替え、ベッツィーなど別の名前を名乗ることができます。男の子にはエストロゲン、女の子にはテストステロンなどの異性ホルモンを、ほとんどの左翼州では8歳から投与できます。

Chapter 1 Present day America

These children still believe in Santa Claus, they should not have such warped sexual education.

　これらの子供たちはまだサンタクロースを信じています。そんな子供たちに、そのような歪んだ性教育を受けさせるべきではありません。

Female breasts can be removed at the age of 16. This is not old enough for children to be able to make informed judgements about their sexuality. The drugs administered often cause the child to become sexually sterile, they can never have children themselves as adults.

　女性の乳房は16歳から切除できます。この年齢では、自分の性に関して十分な知識に基づいて判断を下すことができません。投与される薬物のせいで子供が不妊になることが多く、大人になっても子供を授かることができなくなります。

Primary school libraries have children's books glorifying the joy of changing genders, high school libraries have comics and books teach children how to have gay sex.

　小学校の図書館には性転換の喜びを讃える児童書があり、高校の図書館には同性愛者のセックスのやり方を教える漫画や書籍があります。

Parents often protest these activities by schools at Parent Teacher association meetings. The Biden administration labels them as "Domestic

Terrorists", they are investigated by the FBI to try to find some wrongdoing.

　保護者はPTAの会合で学校のこうした活動に頻繁に抗議しています。バイデン政権は彼らを「国内テロリスト」と呼び、FBIが保護者に違法行為がないか捜査しています。

In California, it is now State law that if parents refuse to provide their child with sex change medical care, it is child abuse. The State of California will confiscate the child and set them up with foster parents. In my studies of history, I have discovered that normally around 6% to 8% of any given population is gay. Yet because of all the proselytizing by the American education system, now some 40% of elementary students in America believe they are LGBT.

　カリフォルニア州では、親が子供の性転換手術を拒否した場合、それは児童虐待であると州法で定められています。カリフォルニア州はその子供を保護し、里親に引き渡します。私は歴史を研究する中で、通常、人口の約6パーセントから8パーセントが同性愛者であることを知りました。しかし、アメリカの教育システムによる布教活動のせいで、現在アメリカの小学生の約40パーセントが自分はLGBTだと信じています。

If a teacher refuses to participate in such activities or protests them, they are fired. For the American radical Left, this is a way to destroy traditional Americans families, and encourage Left-wing revolution in America. For the pharmaceutical industry, it is a source of immense profit.

教師がそのような活動に参加することを拒否したり、抗議したりすると、解雇されます。アメリカの急進左派にとって、これは伝統的なアメリカ人の家庭を破壊し、アメリカで左翼革命を奨励する方法です。製薬業界にとっては、莫大な利益の源泉です。

That these activities cause people extreme harm does not matter at all to the radical Left or the pharmaceutical industry.

こうした活動が人々に甚大な被害を与えても、過激な左翼や製薬業界にとっては知ったことではないのです。

The decline of American power
アメリカのマンパワーの劣化

This has been going on for decades. It has gradually built up into the present mess. The result is that in the present time American weapons have proven greatly inferior to Russian ones. America is having great difficulty in finding engineers to expand artillery production. America has failed at producing a hypersonic missile, while Russia has long been using the Kinzhal missile to great effect.

これは何十年も続いています。それが徐々に積み重なって、現在の混乱に至ったのです。その結果、現在のアメリカ製兵器はロシア製兵器より大幅に劣っていることが証明されてしまいました。アメリカは大砲の生産拡大に必要な技術者を確保するのに大変苦労しています。アメリカは極超音速ミサイルの製造に失敗しましたが、ロ

シアは長年にわたって、キンジャールミサイルを効果的に運用してきました。

America does not have enough welders to produce more than 6 warships next year, while 19 ships are being retired, and the Chinese Navy is expanding.

アメリカには来年 6 隻以上の軍艦を建造するのに必要な溶接工を確保できません。しかし 19 隻の軍艦が退役します。一方、中国海軍は拡大しています。

By the way, the Russian education system has fantastic science and math programs. In America, science has long been performed by foreigners, particularly from China and India. Because of Liberal policies, increasing crime and teaching LGBT education from preschool, these intelligent foreigners have returned to their home countries. They do not wish to have their children brain washed by awful American education.

ちなみに、ロシアの教育制度には優れた科学と数学のプログラムがあります。アメリカでは、科学は長い間、特に中国やインドから来た外国人が担ってきました。リベラルな政策、犯罪の増加、幼稚園からの LGBT 教育のため、これらの知的な外国人は母国に帰りました。彼らは、ひどいアメリカの教育によって子供たちが洗脳されることを望んでいません。

And that is why I have doubts that even a rural America led by the

Chapter 1 Present day America

state of Texas can survive. The electric grid of Texas is in a very poor state. It has come close to collapse several times. There simply are not enough engineers in America to maintain it. If it fails, the future of America will be a hunter/gatherer society, with a population some 10% of what exists now.

　だからこそ、テキサス州が主導するアメリカ農村部でさえ生き残れるかどうか疑問に思うのです。テキサスの電力網は非常に劣悪な状態です。何度も崩壊寸前にまで陥りました。アメリカには電力網を維持できる技術者が足りないのです。電力網が機能しなくなったら、アメリカの将来は狩猟採集社会となり、人口は現在の10パーセント程度になるでしょう。

And such Feminist American women love President Biden, and hate Donald Trump. Joe Biden is old, senile, and weak, dependent on women. For Feminists that is fantastic. On the other hand, even though Donald Trump is 77 years old, he is quite virile and physically strong. Feminists hate that, it reminds them of a strong father.

　そして、そのようなフェミニストのアメリカ人女性はバイデン大統領を愛し、ドナルド・トランプを嫌っています。ジョー・バイデンは年老いており、痴呆症で、弱々しく、女性に頼っています。フェミニストにとってそれは素晴らしいことです。一方、ドナルド・トランプは77歳ですが、非常に男らしく、体力もあります。だからトランプをフェミニストは嫌うのです。強い父親を思い出させるからです。

The mental feebleness of President Biden is obvious to the world. For the Feminists, this is not a problem, as they feel America will in case dominate the world. They ignore the facts that America is indeed falling apart.

　バイデン大統領の精神的な弱さは世界中に知れ渡っています。フェミニストにとってこれは問題ではありません。アメリカはいずれ世界を支配するだろうと彼らは確信しているからです。彼らはアメリカが実際に崩壊しつつあるという事実を無視しています。

Some Japanese women have gone to America and become involved with American Feminists. These American women say that the psychological problems that these Japanese women have are the result of a male dominated society. These Japanese women do not find solutions in America, but only more problems.

　日本人女性の中にはアメリカに渡り、アメリカのフェミニストたちと関わるようになった人もいます。アメリカ人女性たちは、日本人女性が抱える心理的問題は男性優位の社会の結果だと言います。こうした日本人女性たちはアメリカで解決策を見つけるどころか、問題を増やすばかりです。

I remember when I first came to Japan 50 years ago, many Japanese men wanted me to introduce American women to them. I was appalled. Japanese women are so much more feminine than Americans, and dress much better. There used to be a lot of American women in the hostess business, but now, if it is Caucasian women, they are from Eastern Europe. These women are much better mannered than American women.

Chapter 1 Present day America

　50年前に初めて日本に来たとき、多くの日本人男性が私にアメリカ人女性を紹介してほしいと頼んできたことを覚えています。私は愕然としました。日本人女性はアメリカ人女性よりもずっと女性らしく、服装もずっと素敵です。かつてはホステス業に多くのアメリカ人女性がいましたが、今では白人女性といえば東ヨーロッパ出身です。彼女たちはアメリカ人女性よりもずっと礼儀正しいのです。

American business troubles
アメリカのビジネストラブル

Another aspect of American troubles is the Boeing corporation. In March of 2024, a door blew out from the mid fuselage section of an Alaskan Airlines jet. It was a Boeing 737-9 Max aircraft. Miraculously, no one was pulled out of the airplane by decompression or seriously injured.

　アメリカのもう一つの問題は、ボーイング社です。2024年3月、アラスカ航空のジェット機の胴体中央部からドアが吹き飛びました。それはボーイング737-9Max機でした。奇跡的に、減圧によって飛行機から飛び出したり、重傷を負った人はいませんでした。

After the accident, inspections were done at the Boeing Renton Washington factory. It was found that some 50 Boeing 737-9 Max aircraft under construction had mis drilled holes. It was also found that some 300 Boeing 777 had poor electrical installation near a central fuel tank in the aircraft.

第1章　現在のアメリカ

　事故後、ワシントン州レントンにあるボーイング社の工場で検査が行われ、製造中のボーイング737-9Max機約50機に誤った穴あけ加工をしていたことが判明しました。また、ボーイング777機約300機の機体中央燃料タンク付近の電気系統に、施工不良があったことも判明しました。

This could result in a short circuit and spark inside the fuel tank during flight, which would be catastrophic.

　これにより、飛行中に燃料タンク付近でショートして火花が発生し、大惨事につながる可能性があります。

I see three causes for this difficulties with Boeing. There was a lot of pressure from management to speed up production. Also there is a strong pressure to hire people based on their race or sex rather than qualifications. This is diversity hiring. In any case, since American education has declined so steeply since the Vietnam war, there are fewer and fewer people in America who could meet stringent engineering requirements.

　ボーイングのこのトラブルの原因は三つあると私は考えています。経営陣から納期を短縮せよという大きな圧力がありました。また、能力より人種や性別に基づいて雇用せよという強い圧力もありました。いわゆるダイバーシティー（多様性）採用です。そして教育レベルの低下です。ベトナム戦争以来、アメリカの教育レベルは大きく低下しているため、厳しい技術者要件を満たすことができる人材はアメリカではどんどん少なくなっています。

But to American thinking, the most important thing in business is profit. Really, product quality does not factor very much into American thinking. When I first came to Japan, I was amazed to see that Japanese people have so much pride in the products they create, and work so hard for quality. Americans simply do not.

しかし、アメリカ人の考え方では、ビジネスで最も重要なことは利益です。実際、製品の品質は、アメリカ人の考え方ではあまり重視されていません。私が初めて日本に来たとき、日本人が自分たちが作った製品に大きな誇りを持ち、品質向上のために非常に努力しているのを見て驚きました。アメリカ人はそうではありません。

The dystopian future of America
ディストピア化するアメリカ

Life in future America will be dystopian. Let us take a look at what it will be like. In America A, after the waves of refugees to the country side, eventually the population of cities will settle. Gangs themselves will most likely remain in the ruins of the cities, and due to their possessing arms, they will rule them.

未来のアメリカでの生活は、非常にディストピア的なものになるでしょう。それがどのようなものになるか見てみましょう。アメリカ A では、難民の波が田舎に押し寄せた後、最終的に都市の住民が定住します。ギャング自体は都市の廃墟に残る可能性が高く、武器を所有しているため、都市を支配するでしょう。

第1章 現在のアメリカ

The police may maintain control over certain areas of major urban areas, but not all. Actually, this is already happening. In most major American cities there are neighborhoods where police do not go. These are called "no-go" zones.

　警察は大都市の特定の地域を統制しているかもしれませんが、すべてではありません。実際、これはすでに起こっています。アメリカの大都市のほとんどには、警察が立ち入らない地区があります。これらは「立ち入り禁止」ゾーンと呼ばれています。

In these "no-go" zones, gangs would rule, and set whatever laws they wished. Already, in certain cities, there seems to be cooperation between local Black and Hispanic politicians and gangs.

　これらの「立ち入り禁止」ゾーンでは、ギャングが支配し、彼らが望むどんな法律でも制定することになります。すでにいくつかの都市では、地元の黒人やヒスパニック系の政治家とギャングが協力しているようです。

In Northern cities like Chicago or New York, I do not think the gangs will be able to control the suburbs completely. They are mostly White. The problem here is the migrant population. Illegal migrants are mostly Hispanic, and they are distributed everywhere. By the government.

　シカゴやニューヨークのような北部の都市では、ギャングが郊外を完全に支配できるとは思えません。ギャングのほとんどは白人で

Chapter 1 Present day America

す。ここでの問題は移民人口です。不法移民のほとんどはヒスパニック系で、彼らは政府によってあらゆる場所に分散しています。

They are mostly criminals, and have already joined up with local Hispanic gangs. This is really serious. Their main problem will be food supply. Truckers are unlikely to venture into gang ruled cities to deliver food. Already, food thefts are happening from truck stops outside Philadelphia.

　彼らのほとんどは犯罪者で、すでに地元のヒスパニック系ギャングと合流しています。これは本当に深刻です。彼らの主な問題は食糧供給でしょう。トラック運転手がギャングが支配する都市に食糧を配達しに行くことはまずないでしょう。すでにフィラデルフィア

Drug addicts on the streets of Philadelphia

フィラデルフィアの路上でゾンビ化する薬物中毒者ら

第1章　現在のアメリカ

郊外のトラック停留所で食糧窃盗が起きています。

That is one way they can obtain food. Also, drug sales to suburban White communities. The American White population is massively becoming addicted to drugs. Ingredients for the manufacture of Fentanyl is smuggled across the southern border. Labs to manufacture drugs will be set up in abandoned buildings in urban centers.

　それが彼らが食糧を得る方法の一つです。また、郊外の白人コミュニティへの麻薬販売もあります。アメリカの白人は大勢麻薬中毒になっていきます。フェンタニルの製造原料は南の国境を越えて密輸されます。麻薬を製造するための研究所は、都市中心部の廃墟の建物に設置されるでしょう。

Another business between the ruined urban centers and the suburbs will be salvage. As people flee the cities, some buildings will become abandoned, as has happened in Detroit. There will be items of value there, such as copper wiring. America is already suffering from a lack of manufacturing. Items such as copper wiring will become difficult to produce, thus there will be a business to salvage abandoned buildings. Also, usable computers.

　廃墟となった都市中心部と郊外の間で行われるもう一つのビジネスは、廃品の回収です。人々が都市から逃げ出すと、デトロイトのように、いくつかの建物が放棄されます。そこには銅線などの価値のある品物があります。アメリカはすでに製造業の不足に悩まされています。銅線などの品物の生産は困難になるため、放棄された建

Chapter 1 Present day America

物から使えるものを回収するビジネスが生まれます。また、使用可能なコンピューターもあるでしょう。

But it will be a very dangerous business, as these building will no longer be maintained, and floors could collapse. Urban gangs will likely oversee this business, use it to trade for food.

しかし、これらの建物はメンテナンスされなくなり、床が崩壊する可能性があるため、これは非常に危険なビジネスとなるでしょう。都市部のギャングがこのビジネスを監視し、食料との取引に利用する可能性が高いでしょう。

If Kamala Harris and Tim Walz become the leaders of the United States, this is the American future. If it is Donald Trump and J. D. Vance, the future will urban conflict as a future President Trump attempts to clean out illegal migrant gangs. He has promised to deport them if elected President. But their home countries in Central and South America do not want them back. Their crime rates have greatly decreased since they left.

カマラ・ハリス氏とティム・ウォルツ氏が米国のリーダーになれば、これがアメリカの未来です。ドナルド・トランプ氏とJ・D・ヴァンス氏なら、トランプ大統領が不法移民ギャングの一掃を試み、将来は都市紛争になるでしょう。トランプは大統領に選ばれたら彼らを国外追放すると約束しています。しかし、彼らの母国である中南米は彼らの帰国を望んでいません。彼らが国を去ってから犯罪率は大幅に減少しています。

So perhaps a future President Trump will just have to shoot them. In any case an operation to clear out illegal migrants will most likely require military help. This is something Japan should think about by letting in so many migrants.

　だから、おそらく将来のトランプ大統領は彼らを撃つしかないでしょう。いずれにせよ、不法移民を一掃する作戦にはおそらく軍の支援が必要になるでしょう。多くの移民を受けいれている日本は、この点について考えるべきです。

In the above situation, life for Americans in conservative rural states will be near normal. However, ports in major cities, and the airports of major cities, may no longer function because of criminal activity.

　上記の状況では、保守的な田舎の州に住むアメリカ人の生活はほぼ正常になります。しかし、犯罪行為により、大都市の港や空港は機能しなくなる可能性があります。

Much more serious is America B. For decades, most of America's scientists and engineers have been foreigners. Intelligent Americans would seek careers in finance. Now, because of increased crime, and poor schools, these engineers and scientists are returning to the countries of their origin.

　さらに深刻なのはアメリカBです。何十年もの間、アメリカの科学者やエンジニアのほとんどは外国人でした。賢いアメリカ人は金融業界でのキャリアを求めていました。しかし、現在、犯罪の増

Chapter 1 Present day America

加と学校の質の悪さから、これらのエンジニアや科学者は母国に帰国しています。

They do not wish to live in America and have their children educated into become transgender. And schools only teach about suppression of racial minorities and LGBT. So we have an entire generation of scientifically illiterate Americans, and we no longer have foreign engineers to fill the gaps.

　彼らはアメリカに住んで、子供たちがトランスジェンダーになるように教育されることを望んでいません。そして学校では人種的マイノリティとLGBTの抑圧についてしか教えていません。そのため、科学的に無知なアメリカ人が全世代を占め、そのギャップを埋める外国人エンジニアはもういません。

If Donald Trump regains the Presidency, he intends to drastically reform American education. But it will take between 20 or 30 years before we can see results. 90% of American educators are leftists, and they will strongly oppose any such effort by a future President Trump.

　ドナルド・トランプ氏が大統領に復帰すれば、彼はアメリカの教育を抜本的に改革するつもりです。しかし、結果が見られるようになるまでには20年から30年かかるでしょう。アメリカの教育者の90%は左派であり、彼らは将来のトランプ大統領によるそのような取り組みに強く反対するでしょう。

If Kamala Harris becomes President, things will continue in education as they have been, and become much worse.

　カマラ・ハリス氏が大統領になれば、教育の状況はこれまで通り続き、さらに悪化するでしょう。

It may become impossible to maintain an electric grid across the entire United States. When things break, it requires technically able people to maintain them, and America lacks such skilled people.

　アメリカ全土の電力網を維持するのは不可能になるかもしれません。何かが壊れたら、それを維持できる技術を持った人材が必要ですが、アメリカにはそうした熟練した人材が不足しています。

In this case, America will decline into a nation of subsistence farming, and roaming hunters, living off pigs and cows that have gone wild. In such a case, CIA studies imagine that population of the United States will decline by 90%. Only the most physically hardy people will survive.

　この場合、アメリカは自給自足の農業と放浪狩猟民の国に衰退し、野生化した豚や牛を食べて暮らすことになります。そのような場合、CIAの調査では、米国の人口は90パーセント減少すると予測されています。最も肉体的に丈夫な人々だけが生き残るでしょう。

Two thirds of Americans are seriously overweight, in such an America, they will not survive.

Chapter 1 Present day America

アメリカ人の３分の２は深刻な肥満であり、そのようなアメリカでは彼らは生き残れないでしょう。

Elon Musk's personal tragedy
イーロン・マスクの悲劇

Recently, Elon Musk has moved his Corporate headquarters from Hawthorn California to his space base in Texas. I have always been a fan of Elon Musk. I was thrilled when he successfully built rockets that can launch objects into space, and then return to earth to be reused again. This is revolutionary in space travel.

最近、イーロン・マスク氏は本社をカリフォルニア州ホーソンからテキサス州の宇宙基地に移転しました。私はずっとイーロン・マスク氏のファンでした。彼が宇宙に物体を打ち上げ、その後地球に戻って再利用できるロケットの開発に成功したときは感激しました。これは宇宙旅行における革命です。

Elon Musk
イーロン・マスク

But the move from California is not about space. It is about Transgenderism. Recently, he lost his son to the Transgender movement. The son has changed into a woman, and filed legal paperwork to keep his father away. The child is presently 20 years old.

しかし、カリフォルニアからの移住は、スペースの問題ではありません。トランスジェンダーの問題です。最近、彼はトランスジェンダー運動のせいで息子を失いました。息子は女性に性転換し、父親を遠ざけるために法的書類を提出しました。現在、その子供は20歳です。

Elon Musk at first believed his son's school when teachers and administrators told him that if his son could not transition into a woman, he would commit suicide. In California, if the parents do not agree to this for their teenage children, the state will take the child away from the parents and put him or her under the care of the state.

イーロン・マスク氏は、教師や学校関係者から、息子が女性に性転換できなければ自殺するだろうと言われた際、最初は息子の学校の言うことを信じていました。カリフォルニア州では、親が十代の子供の性転換に同意しない場合、州は子供を親から引き離し、州の保護下に置くことになります。

Medical professionals, school teachers and administrators in America all put pressure on all children to change their sex medically. They are paid by the pharmaceutical industry to do this.

Chapter 1 Present day America

アメリカの医療専門家、学校の教師、行政関係者は皆、すべての子供たちに医学的に性別を変えるよう圧力をかけています。それで彼らは製薬業界から報酬を受け取っています。

These treatments are medically irreversible, and in the case of hormone and puberty blocking treatments, result in sterilization of the individual concerned. Children, many of them at an age where they still believe in Santa Claus, cannot possibly comprehend what this means for their future when they agree to such treatments.

これらの治療は医学的に不可逆的であり、ホルモン治療や思春期阻害治療の場合、対象者の不妊化につながります。サンタクロースの存在をまだ信じている年齢の子供たちの多くは、このような治療に同意しても、それが自分たちの将来にどのような意味を持つのか理解できないでしょう。

By pushing these treatments onto children, the American medical and pharmaceutical industries have shown themselves to be criminals, concerned only with profit, and not the well being of the people of the nation. These kind of policies are happening in all Blue, liberal states. In the Red, conservative states, people are fighting to save their children from such a Hell.

こうした治療を子供たちに押し付けることによって、アメリカの医療業界と製薬業界は、利益だけを気にし、国民の幸福など考えていない犯罪者であることを露呈しました。こうした政策は、青の(民主党支持が多い)リベラルな州すべてで行われています。赤の(共

第 1 章　現在のアメリカ

和党支持が多い）保守的な州では、人々は子供たちをそのような地獄から救うために戦っています。

So Elon Musk moves his corporation from California to Texas. California loses all that tax money and those people. Actually, many Americans are making the same move, so many that California is considering creating a departure tax. California has become an extreme Left-wing state, riddled with crime and homelessness. It is a total Left-wing mistake.

　そこでイーロン・マスク氏は会社をカリフォルニアからテキサスに移転します。カリフォルニアは税収を失い、雇用も失います。実際、多くのアメリカ人が同じように逃げ出しており、あまりに多いためカリフォルニアは出州税の導入を検討しています。カリフォルニアは犯罪とホームレスが蔓延する極左の州になってしまいました。これは完全に左翼の間違いです。

Former President Trump rallies again with Elon Musk at the site of the assassination attempt (Butler, Pennsylvania)
イーロン・マスクと 暗殺未遂現場で再び集会するトランプ前大統領（ペンシルベニア州バトラー）

Chapter 2 The American future
第2章 アメリカの未来

Donald Trump and the elections
ドナルド・トランプと選挙

The United States likes to present itself as the world's greatest democracy. But this is now far from the truth. Let us look in detail at what has happened in the last few years.

　アメリカは自らを世界で最も偉大な民主主義国家であるかのように見せたがります。しかし、それは今や真実からかけ離れています。ここ数年、何が起こったのかを詳しく見てみましょう。

However, the 2020 Presidential election was a farce. There were millions of mail-in ballots that were fake. Many foreigners were given the right to vote by Democratic activists. Criticizing or protesting the fraudulent election has become a crime.

　2020年の大統領選挙は茶番劇でした。偽造された郵便投票が何百万通もありました。民主党活動家によって多くの外国人に投票権が与えられました。不正選挙を批判したり抗議したりすることは犯罪となりました。

Some 277 people have gone to prison for demonstrating against the election fraud in Washington DC on January 6 2024. Most of them were simply arrested but never received a trial. For three years, they have languished in prison.

2024年1月6日にワシントンD.C.で行われた選挙不正に抗議するデモに参加した約277人が刑務所に送られました。彼らのほとんどは逮捕されましたが、裁判を受けることはありませんでした。彼らは3年間、刑務所で苦しみ続けています。

Donald Trump

(45th President of the United States)

ドナルド・トランプ
(第45代アメリカ合衆国大統領)

The Democrats simply said they tried to make an insurrection. What really happened is that Trump supporters simply voiced doubts about the election, and wanted it to be investigated and confirmed. In a democracy, this is no crime. Where freedom of speech exists, in a democracy, there is every right to confirm the results of an election. It is not a crime. Calling it a crime only happens in totalitarian regimes.

民主党は、彼らが「暴動を起こそうとした」と主張しました。しかし実際に起こったのは、トランプ支持者が選挙に疑念を持ち、それを調査し確認することを求めただけです。民主主義では、これは犯罪ではありません。言論の自由が存在する民主主義では、選挙結果を確認する権利は十分にあります。これは犯罪ではありません。

Chapter 2 The American future

これを犯罪と呼ぶのは全体主義体制においてのみ起こることです。

In fact, security camera footage caught election workers handling fake ballots after observers had left. In other places, observers were physically barred from polling places. Countless illegal events happened. On January 6, 2021, former Army General Michael Flynn offered to have the United States military redo the election if President Trump would declare martial law.

　実際、監視カメラの映像には、立会人が去った後、選挙管理員が偽の投票用紙を扱っている姿が映っていました。別の場所では、立会人が投票所から物理的に締め出されました。違法な出来事が数え切れないほど起きていました。2021年1月6日、マイケル・フリン元陸軍大将は、トランプ大統領が戒厳令を宣言するなら、アメリカ軍に選挙をやり直させると申し出ました。

President Trump declined the offer. I think he did not want to plunge the nation into civil war. But I think this only delayed the conflict. And we should look at the obvious. For a year before the election, during the campaign, both Joe Biden and Donald Trump made many campaign appearances. Joe Biden drew an average crowd of 12 people. I remember one event in Arizona where not one person came. He spent most of the campaign in his basement.

　トランプ大統領はこの申し出を断りました。彼は内戦を引き起こしたくなかったのだと思います。しかし、これは内戦を遅らせただけだと思います。そして、私たちは明白な事実に目を向けるべきで

す。選挙前の1年間の選挙期間中、バイデン氏もトランプ氏も選挙運動に姿を現しました。バイデン氏は平均12人の観衆を集めました。アリゾナ州でのイベントには1人も来なかったことを覚えています。彼は選挙戦のほとんどを自宅の地下室で過ごしました。

Donald Trump would get an enthusiastic crowd that was usually around 40,000 people. Yet we are supposed to believe that Joe Biden won the Presidency with 81 million votes, the most of any candidate in history. And to question this is a crime? America is most certainly no longer a democracy.

　トランプ氏には、通常4万人ほどの熱狂的な観衆が集まります。しかし、私たちはバイデン氏が8100万票という史上最多の得票数で大統領選に勝利したと信じなければならないのです。これに疑問を呈することは犯罪ですか？　アメリカはもはや民主主義国家ではありません。

The criminal cases against Donald Trump
トランプ前大統領に対する裁判

Donald Trump is drawing large crowds at rallies, even among Black and Hispanic voters, who traditionally vote Democrat. Thus, the Democratic establishment has devised a new tactic to destroy Donald Trump. That is called "Lawfare". This is a new term combining the words law and warfare. It means to use the law as a weapon.

　ドナルド・トランプ氏は、伝統的に民主党に投票する黒人やヒ

Chapter 2　The American future

スパニック系の有権者も、大勢集会に集めています。そこで民主党は、ドナルド・トランプ氏を潰す新しい戦術を考案しました。それが「ローフェア」です。これは、法律と戦争という言葉を組み合わせた新しい言葉です。法律を武器として使うことを意味します。

Well, law was never intended to be used as a weapon. In fact, the concept of using law to settle disputes instead of warfare is meant to preserve civilization. By engaging in this "Lawfare", Democrats have dameged the American legal system.

　法律は武器として使うことを意図したものではありません。実際、紛争を解決するために戦争ではなく法律を用いるという概念は、文明を守るためのものです。この「ローフェア」を実行することで、民主党はアメリカの法制度に害をもたらしました。

In Georgia, Donald Trump was charged by District Attorney Fani Willis with doubting 2020 election results. However, this is not a crime, and the legal case has basically collapsed due to her misconduct.

　ジョージア州では、ドナルド・トランプ氏が2020年の選挙結果を疑ったとして、ファニ・ウィリス地方検事から訴追されました。しかし、これは犯罪ではなく、彼女の不正行為によってこの訴訟は基本的に破綻しています。

In New York City, Letitia James charged Donald Trump with falsifying the value of his property in business negotiations. A Democratic judge ordered him to pay an immense fine. It was more than he could pay, and the court began moves to confiscate his property. But this is not a crime, and a higher court reduced the charges, and the legal case has faded from the news.

ニューヨーク市では、レティシア・ジェームズ氏がトランプ氏をビジネス交渉において財産の価値を偽ったとして告訴しました。民主党の判事はトランプ氏に巨額の罰金の支払いを命じました。それはトランプ氏の支払い能力を超えるもので、裁判所はトランプ氏の財産を没収する手続きを開始しました。しかしこれは犯罪ではなく、上級裁判所が罪を軽減したため、この訴訟はニュースから消えていきました。

Finally, in late May, in a legal case filed by District Attorney Alvin Bragg, Donald Trump was found guilty of falsifying business records. The accusation was that he paid "hush money" to a porn star with whom he alleged to have had sex, in order to hide a potentially damaging incident that could affect his Presidential campaign.

最終的に、5月下旬、アルビン・ブラッグ地方検事が起こした訴訟で、トランプ氏は業務記録の偽造で有罪となりました。告発内容は、トランプ氏が大統領選挙運動に影響を与える可能性のある不祥事を隠すために、性的関係を持ったとされるセクシー女優に「口止め料」を支払ったというものでした。

Again, this is not a crime. On July 11, he will be sentenced, and he could spend up to 30 days in jail. Some Democratic lawmakers in Congress are attempting to remove Donald Trump from Secret Service protection, due to his status as a convicted felon.

　もう一度言いますが、これは犯罪ではありません。7月11日に判決が下され、最長30日間刑務所に収監される可能性があります。議会には、トランプ氏が有罪判決を受けたため、シークレットサービスの保護から外そうとしている民主党議員もいます。

The sentencing has since been extended again until November 26, after the election. There is no news on possible penalties Judge Merchan may impose, or if he will extend the sentencing further.

　判決は選挙後の11月26日まで再び延長されました。マーチャン判事が科す可能性のある刑罰や、判決をさらに延長するかどうかについては、何も報道されていません。

Rumors are that he could be sent to Rikers Island, a prison in New York City that is very dangerous. It is becoming increasingly obvious that this is an attempt to assassinate Donald Trump.

　噂によると、彼はライカーズ島（ニューヨーク市にある非常に危険な刑務所）に送られるかもしれないとのことです。これはトランプ氏を暗殺するためのものであることが明らかになりつつあります。

All of the above legal cases are not crimes. This is the new America: if the government does not like you, they can destroy you. Regarding the case brought by Letitia James, ordinary Americans have reacted.

　上記の訴訟はすべて犯罪ではありません。これが新しいアメリカです。政府があなたを気に入らなければ、あなたを潰すことができます。レティシア・ジェームズ氏の訴訟に関して、普通のアメリカ人は反応しました。

In New York State in February of 2024, Prosecutor Letitia James and Judge Engoron ruled that Donald Trump must pay 355 million dollars, charging that he committed fraud by overestimating the value of his real estate used as loan collateral.

　トランプ氏が融資のための担保不動産の資産価値を過大に見積もる不正を働いたとして、ニューヨークのレティシア・ジェームズ州司法長官が提訴した民事訴訟で、2024年2月、ニューヨーク州地裁のエンゴロン判事はドナルド・トランプ氏に3億5,500万ドルを支払うよう命じました。

Despite New York State Governor Kathy Hochul's assurances to investors that their money was safe, this was simply an attack on Donald Trump; consequently investors began to leave New York City to invest in Florida, Texas, and Nevada.

　ニューヨーク州のキャシー・ホークル知事は、これは単にトランプ氏に対する攻撃であり、投資家の資金は安全であると保証したにもかかわらず、投資家はニューヨークを離れ、フロリダ、テキサス、

Chapter 2 The American future

ネバダに投資し始めました。

In this New York State court case against Donald Trump, The Accusations of racism in store closings against Boston Walgreens, Mayor Johnson's plan to build city run grocery stores, Leftist politicians and officials have shown themselves to be blinded by ideology. They cannot understand reality.

　トランプ氏に対するニューヨークの裁判、ボストン・ウォルグリーンの店舗閉鎖における人種差別の告発、シカゴのジョンソン市長の市営食料品店建設計画など、左派の政治家や役人たちは、イデオロギーに盲目であることを示しています。彼らは現実を理解できません。

In fact, Left-wing politicians are ramping up their activities. Concerning the decline of degradation that have befallen most large American cities, one city I have not mentioned is Boston. Until now. Mayor Michelle Wu, a Chinese American who was elected in 2021, has decided to decriminalize centain offenses.

　実際、左翼政治家の活動は活発化しています。アメリカのほとんどの大都市に見られる衰退の傾向について、私が言及しなかった都市が一つあります。それはボストンです。しかしボストンにおいても、2021年に当選した中国系アメリカ人のミシェル・ウー市長は、犯罪の非犯罪化を決定しました。

Shoplifting, breaking and entering, property destruction, larceny under $250 are no longer considered crimes. She also started that any police officers who participated in the January 2021 pro-Trump demonstrations should be fired, and police computer data bases on criminals destroyed.

万引き、不法侵入、器物損壊、250ドル以下の窃盗はもはや犯罪ではありません。彼女はまた、2021年1月のトランプ支持デモに参加した警察官は全員解雇すべきであり、犯罪者に関する警察のコンピューター・データベースは破棄すべきだと述べました。

This is insane. Has she really not seen the damage such liberal policies have done to San Francisco, Chicago, and New York? I am sure she has, it is on the news, it is impossible not to notice. So why does she protect criminals and encourage crime?

正気の沙汰とは思えません。彼女は、このようなリベラルな政策がサンフランシスコ、シカゴ、ニューヨークに何をもたらしたか見たことがないのでしょうか？　ニュースになっているのだから、気づかないはずがありません。それなのに、なぜ彼女は犯罪者を保護し、犯罪を助長するのでしょうか？

The truck drivers strike
トラックドライバーによるストライキ

American freight moves by truck. 70% is by truck, 30% is by rail. Almost all American truckers are independent operators. They are mostly conservative, and Trump supporters. When Letitia James announced her fine and intention to confiscate Donald Trump's property, they declared a strike, starting they would not deliver goods to New York City.

アメリカの貨物はトラックで運ばれます。70パーセントはトラック、30パーセントは鉄道です。アメリカのトラック運転手はほぼ全員が個人事業主です。彼らはほとんどが保守派で、トランプ支持者です。レティシア・ジェームズ氏がトランプ氏への罰金と財産没収の意向を発表すると、彼らはストライキを宣言し、ニューヨーク市への貨物の配送を拒否しました。

Although only 22% of American truckers have participated in the strike, but this has caused serious price increases in New York City. What is even more damaging is the loss of business investment. Investors saw this abuse of the law by Democrats, and became worried. New York State Governor Kathy Hochul tried to reassure worried investors that they would be safe, claiming this was only a tactic to take down Donald Trump.

アメリカのトラック運転手のうち、ストライキに参加したのは22パーセントに過ぎませんが、ニューヨーク市では深刻な物価上昇を引き起こしました。それよりも深刻なのは、企業の投資損失です。投資家たちは民主党によるこの法律の濫用を見て、不安になりました。ニューヨーク州のキャシー・ホークル知事は、これはトランプ氏を潰すためのものに過ぎない、とそんな投資家たちを安心させようとしました。

第 2 章　アメリカの未来

Investors were not reassured, and many have fled the New York City investment market for Miami or Austin. These legal actions have seriously damaged New York City. However, now there is the possibility of Donald Trump actually being arrested and imprisoned.

　投資家たちは安心できず、多くがニューヨーク市の投資市場からマイアミやオースティンに逃げ出しました。これらの法的措置はニューヨーク市に深刻なダメージを与えました。しかし、今やドナルド・トランプ氏が実際に逮捕され、投獄される可能性が出てきました。

This has led many commentators to express open concerns online that Civil War could be the result of such a move. I think that is possible,

Group of people with "STOP OFFSHORING" posters

"海外移転するな" とポスターで抗議する人々

135

but even if war does not happen, civil disorder will result.

　このため、多くの論者がネット上で公然と、このような動きの結果、内戦が起きるのではないかと懸念しています。私はその可能性はあると思いますが、たとえ内戦は起こらなくても、騒乱は起きるでしょう。

America has declined so much that it has become a developing country.

　アメリカは衰退の一途をたどり、第三世界の国になってしまいました。

However, at the beginning of July, the Supreme Court ruled the President has immunity for official acts. Whether that would apply to the New York case, I do not know, I am not a lawyer.

　しかし、7月初旬、最高裁判所は大統領には公務上の行為に対する免責特権があるとの判決を下しました。それがニューヨークの事件に適用されるかどうかは、私は弁護士ではないので分かりません。

Judge Merchan then extended the sentencing until September 18, then "only if necessary". Which implies this the case may be dropped entirely. It has since been further extended until November 26.

　マーチャン判事はその後、判決を9月18日まで延長し、その後は「必要な場合のみ」としました。これは、訴訟が完全に取り下げ

られる可能性があることを意味しています。判決はその後さらに 11 月 26 日まで延長されました。

The greed of the Democrats
利己主義を極めるアメリカ民主党

There is much evidence of the criminality of the Biden family, including the President himself. Yet there are no investigations. The existence of the Hunter Biden laptop, long held by the FBI, has finally been comfirmed. In it Hunter is shown doing illegal drugs and having sex with minors. Despite his lack of any qualifications, he held a highly paying job with a Ukrainian energy company, Burisma. He is finally on trial for illegal possession of a firearm.

　大統領自身を含むバイデン一家の犯罪行為を示す証拠はたくさんあります。しかし、捜査は行われていません。FBI が長い間保管していたハンター・バイデン氏のノートパソコンが本物であることがついに認められました。そこには、ハンター氏が違法薬物を使用し、未成年と性交している様子が映っています。何の資格もないのに、彼はウクライナのエネルギー会社ブリスマで高給の職に就いていました。ようやく彼は銃器不法所持の罪で裁判にかけられることになりました。

While chasing Donald Trump for nonexistent crimes, the American Department of Justice has completely ignored the Biden family. In America, they are called the "Biden Crime Family".

Chapter 2 The American future

　アメリカ司法省は、ありもしない犯罪でトランプ氏を追い詰める一方で、バイデン一家は無視しています。アメリカでは、彼らは「バイデン犯罪ファミリー」と呼ばれています。

Now, with the obvious popularity of Donald Trump, Democrats fear a Trump victory in November. Congressman Adam Schiff, Congresswoman Alexandria Ocasio Cortez, and many other Democratic officials think that Donald Trump will put them in prison in his new term if he wins.

　現在、トランプ氏の人気は明らかで、民主党は11月のトランプ勝利を恐れています。アダム・シフ下院議員、アレクサンドリア・オカシオ・コルテス下院議員、その他多くの民主党関係者は、トランプ氏が勝利すれば、新任期中に自分たちは刑務所に送られることになると考えています。

So they will do anything they can to stop him. Japan is a rational country. The Japanese race and language are everything. America is not, it is a country without a unified race, only partially united by one language. So America created a strong rule of law to rule this disparate country. This was quite necessary, and for a time, it worked well.

　だから彼らは、彼を阻止するためにできることは何でもするでしょう。日本は理性的な国です。日本は長い歴史が有り、皆が同じ言葉を喋り、共通の常識があります。アメリカはそうではありません。真の民族といえるものはなく、一つの言語で部分的に統一されているだけです。だからアメリカはこのバラバラの国を統治するた

めに強力な法の支配を作りました。これは極めて必要なことであり、一時期うまく機能しました。

But for selfish reasons, basically personal greed and lust for power, the Democratic Party has distorted the rule of law, and created a legal system that serves them personally to the detriment of other political factions. This is the death of America as we know it.

しかし、利己的な理由、要するに個人的な欲望と権力欲のために、民主党は法の支配を歪め、他の政党を犠牲にして自分たちに都合のいい法制度を作り上げました。これが、私たちが知っているアメリカの終焉です。

The Trump and Biden debate
トランプとバイデンの討論

On June 28, a debate was held between President Biden and Donald Trump. President Biden's performance was a disaster. Panic is running through the Democratic party.

6月28日、バイデン大統領とトランプ前大統領の討論会が行われました。バイデン大統領のパフォーマンスは散々でした。民主党内にパニックが広がっています。

What the Democrats have long been working so hard to hide, the fact of President Biden's serious Alzheimer's disease, became openly apparent to America and the world.

Chapter 2　The American future

　民主党が長い間ひた隠しにしていた、バイデン大統領が深刻なアルツハイマー病を患っているという事実が、アメリカと世界に対して公然と明らかになりました。

America is led by a man who cannot think and comprehend what is happening around him. We must also question the intelligence of so many Americans of the Democratic party who believe and follow this man.

　アメリカは、自分の周りで何が起こっているのか理解も考察もできない人物に導かれています。私たちはまた、この人物に賛同して従う民主党支持者たちの知性にも疑問を持たなければなりません。

Is it safe for Japan to bet its future on country where the leader is a mumbling old man? I do not think so. What does this tell us about Japanese Prime Minister Kishida? Nothing good.

　指導者が意味不明なことをつぶやく老人である国に日本が将来を賭けるのは安全なことでしょうか？　私はそうは思いません。これは日本の岸田首相について、我々に何を示しているのでしょうか？
　良いことは何もないということです。

Immediately after the debate, many Democrats said that President Biden should be replaced, a new Presidential candidate should be found.

　討論会の直後、多くの民主党員はバイデン大統領を交代させ、新たな大統領候補を見つけるべきだと述べました。

But the rules of the Democratic party are such that, unless President Biden decides to quit himself, he cannot be replaced. Former President Obama supports him, along with the President's wife.

しかし、民主党の規則では、バイデン大統領が自ら辞任を決意しない限り、後任を立てることができません。オバマ元大統領は、大統領夫人とともにバイデン大統領を支持しています。

It seems that the power brokers of the Democratic Party want to keep Joe Biden as the Presidential nominee no matter what. They simply cannot see reality.

民主党の権力者たちは、何があろうともバイデン氏を大統領候補に据えておきたいようです。彼らはまったく現実が見えていません。

The longer they take to replace Joe Biden, the worse it is. The new nominee for President will have less time to campaign and prepare for a possible Presidency. So what is the plan, another pandemic with massive mail-in voter ballot fraud?

バイデン大統領の後任を決めるのが遅れれば遅れるほど、状況は悪くなります。新大統領候補は選挙活動や大統領就任に向けた準備に費やす時間が少なくなります。では何か計画しているのでしょうか。新たなパンデミックを引き起こし、また大規模な郵送投票による不正を仕掛けるのでしょうか？

I don't think that will work so well a second time, the America Right

Chapter 2 The American future

is angry, and it has many weapons. They have the military ability to defeat the American Federal military, and the Federal military would splinter in such a catastrophic event.

　二度目はそううまくいくとは思えません。アメリカ右派は怒っており、多くの武器を持っています。彼らにはアメリカ連邦軍を倒す軍事力があり、そうした重大な事態が発生すれば連邦軍は分裂するでしょう。

But so many Left-wing Americans are so delusional, after all, they believe that a man can become a woman simply by self-declaration.

　しかし、多くの左翼アメリカ人は妄想を抱いています。そもそも彼らは、男性がただ宣言するだけで女性になれると信じているくらいです。

These people are driving the Democratic party to ruin and America along with it. America faces so many difficult challenges. The Ukraine war is going so very badly, American mistakes have killed many Russian civilians, and the Russians are out for revenge. In any case Russia is openly winning the war.

　こうした人々が民主党を破滅に追い込み、アメリカをも滅亡に導こうとしているのです。アメリカは多くの困難な課題に直面しています。ウクライナ戦争は極めて深刻な状況にあり、アメリカの過ちにより多くのロシア市民が命を落とし、ロシアは復讐に燃えています。いずれにせよ、ロシアは戦争で明らかに勝利しています。

第 2 章　アメリカの未来

Saudi Arabia is now buying weapons from the Chinese. The oil dollar has been destroyed, and this will gradually seriously damage the American economy. America has lost the Middle East.

　サウジアラビアは現在、中国から武器を購入しています。ペトロダラーは崩壊し、これが徐々にアメリカ経済に深刻なダメージを与えるでしょう。アメリカは中東を失いました。

The Japanese nation must really step back from this self inflicted American disaster, otherwise Japan could be destroyed along with America.

　日本国民は、アメリカが自ら招いたこの災厄から身を引かなければなりません。さもなければ、日本はアメリカと一緒に滅びてしまうかもしれません。

Biden a mere puppet
操り人形・バイデン

So, who is running the country? That is a very serious question, I would say Barack Obama, but apparently it is a group of aides from Obama, Bernie Sanders and Elizabeth Warren who are deeply committed Leftists that control policy.

　誰がこの国を運営しているのでしょうか？　これは非常に深刻な問題です。私ならバラク・オバマ氏と答えますが、どうやら政策を

Chapter 2　The American future

コントロールしているのはオバマ氏、バーニー・サンダース氏、エリザベス・ウォーレン氏といった側近たちで、彼らは非常に左翼的な考えを持つグループです。

If President Biden were to step down because of age, all these staffers would lose their jobs. Thus they strongly supported him, despite his obvious frailties.

　もしバイデン大統領が高齢を理由に退任すれば、スタッフ全員が職を失うことになります。だから彼らは、バイデン大統領が明らかに衰弱しているにもかかわらず、彼を強く支持していました。

Biden's feebleness has been on display for a long time, but only now does the media pretend to have noticed. And many politicians still support him, but overall, he seems to have lost so many big donors, he may have funding problems.

　バイデン大統領の非力さは以前から明らかでしたが、メディアは今になってようやくそれに気づいたふりをしています。多くの政治家がまだ彼を支持していますが、全体的に見ると、彼は大口寄付者の多くを失ったようで、資金面で問題を抱えているのかもしれません。

And of course, voters are angry, abandoning the Democratic party.

　そしてもちろん、有権者は怒り、民主党を見捨てています。

Prime Minister Kishida, who has met President Biden many times, never noticed anything wrong? Did he feel it was best for Japan to be deeply allied with a country led by a frail senile leader?

　バイデン大統領と何度も会っている岸田首相は、何もおかしいとは思わなかったのでしょうか？　虚弱な老人が率いる国と日本が深い同盟関係を結ぶことが最善だと思ったのでしょうか？

The longer this goes on, the worse it will be, and it could even destroy the Democratic party.

　この状態が長く続くほど、事態は悪化し、民主党を崩壊させる可能性さえあります。

Then there is the agenda, project 2025, for the Republican party. It is a list of things that President Trump should do if he becomes President next January 20th. It was created by Conservatives at the Heritage Foundation.

　それから、共和党のウィッシュリスト「プロジェクト2025」があります。これは、トランプ候補が来年1月20日に大統領に就任した場合に行うべきことのリストです。これはヘリテージ財団の保守派によって作成されました。

He would drastically reform the FBI. Many career bureaucrats would be fired and replaced by government appointees.

Chapter 2 The American future

　彼はFBIを抜本的に改革するでしょう。多くのキャリア官僚が解雇され、政府の任命した人物に置き換えられるでしょう。

The Department of Education would be drastically reformed, all gender and diversity education would be eliminated.

　教育省は大幅に改革され、性別と多様性に関する教育はすべて中止されるでしょう。

A wall will be continued on the U.S-Mexican border.

　アメリカとメキシコの国境に壁が建設され続けるでしょう。

The Left will be sure to fight against this with all their power. They believe that a Trump administration will imprison them or kill them.

　左翼は全力でこれに対抗するでしょう。彼らはトランプ政権が自分たちを投獄するか、殺すだろうと信じています。

Yet in all major cities in America, safety is in rapid decline. Homeless encampments are everywhere. In New York City, The Venezuelan gang, Tren de Arugua has guns in the migrant shelters. In Chicago, if you call the police over a murder, assault or home invasion, there is a 50% chance that the police will not respond for hours. In Los Angeles, young gang members regularly taken over the streets, engaging in dangerous illegal races and shootings.

しかし、アメリカの主要都市では、安全性が急速に低下しています。ホームレスのたむろする場所が至る所に見られます。ニューヨーク市では、ベネズエラのギャング、トレン・デ・アラグアが移民シェルターに銃を隠し持っています。シカゴでは、殺人、暴行、住居侵入で警察に通報しても、警察が何時間も対応しない可能性が50%あります。ロサンゼルスでは、若いギャングのメンバーが定期的に通りを占拠し、危険な違法レースや銃撃事件が発生しています。

If President Trump does win a new term, he may have to declare nationwide martial law. And the Left will resist him.

トランプ大統領が再選されれば、全国に戒厳令を布告せざるを得なくなるかもしれません。そして左派は抵抗するでしょう。

Either way, there is nothing Japan can do to help America. We must help and save Japan.

いずれにせよ、日本がアメリカを助けるためにできることは何もありません。私たちは日本を助け、救わなければなりません。

The Trump assassination attempt
トランプ暗殺未遂事件

Former President Trump was shot by a local man at a political rally in Western Pennsylvania. The former President turned his head at the moment of the shooting, and the bullet merely grazed his ear instead in entering his brain.

トランプ前大統領はペンシルベニア州西部の政治集会で地元の男に銃撃されました。銃撃の瞬間に前大統領は顔をそむけたため、銃弾は脳に撃ち込まれることなく耳ををかすめただけでした。

He was saved by a miracle.

彼は奇跡的に助かりました。

The shooter was then engaged by Secret Service snipers, and killed immediately. He was swiftly identified as Thomas Matthew Crooks, a 20-years-old. He was a local resident.

シークレットサービスの狙撃手に銃撃され、即死しました。犯人はトーマス・マシュー・クルックス、20歳とすぐに特定されました。犯人は地元住民でした。

At this writing, there is no evidence that he had any accomplices; he acted alone. He had no military or apparent job experience. In high school, he was a loner, often bullied by other students. He often dressed in military-style uniforms.

本稿執筆時点では、共犯者がいたという証拠はなく、彼は単独で行動していました。彼には軍隊経験も、明らかな職歴もありませんでした。高校時代、彼は孤独で、他の生徒からよくいじめられてい

ました。彼はよく軍服を着ていました。

There was no apparent conspiracy, just one man. There is a perversity in the American character, where a lone misfit, who does not fit into normal society, chooses to kill a famous person. He did not have any particular passions in life; he was a registered Republican, but donated to Left-leaning Democratic causes.

　明白な陰謀は存在せず、ただ一人の男が犯行に及んだだけです。アメリカ人の性格には倒錯があり、普通の社会に馴染めない孤独なはみ出し者が有名人を殺害することを選びます。彼は人生において特に情熱を傾けるものを持っておらず、共和党員として登録していましたが左派民主党の活動に寄付していました。

Simply, the former President came to speak in his town, so he took the opportunity to attempt to kill him. It seems nothing in his life had any special meaning for him, so he went and did it. Actually, there are many such people in America.

　簡単に言えば、前大統領が彼の町に演説に来たので、彼はその機会を利用して彼を殺そうとしたのです。彼の人生には何も大切なものなどなかったようで、彼はそれを実行したのです。実際、アメリカにはそのような人がたくさんいます。

John Hinckley who shot President Reagan in 1981 was such a person, Mark Chapman who shot John Lennon in 1980 was another. They do not care about caught or killed. From the viewpoint of law enforcement,

Chapter 2　The American future

it is very difficult to stop such an individual.

　1981年にレーガン大統領を射殺したジョン・ヒンクリーもそうだったし、1980年にジョン・レノンを射殺したマーク・チャップマンもそうでした。彼らは捕まるか殺されるかなんて気にしません。法執行機関の観点からすると、そのような人物を止めるのは非常に難しいです。

However, there were major blunders by law enforcement, especially the Secret Service. The rooftop where the shooter fired from was only 150 meters or so from where the former President was standing. Nobody had it under surveillance. The shooter was noticed by bystanders, who alerted police; the police response was one of surprise. Nobody engaged the shooter until he started shooting.

　しかし、警察、特にシークレットサービスによる大きな失策がありました。銃撃犯が発砲した屋上は、前大統領が立っていた場所からわずか150メートルほどしか離れていませんでした。誰も監視していませんでした。銃撃犯は通行人に気づかれ、警察に通報されましたが、警察の対応は驚くべきものでした。銃撃犯が発砲するまで、誰も銃撃犯に対処しようとしませんでした。

One speech attendee was killed, two seriously wounded.

　演説の聴衆1人が死亡し2人が重傷を負いました。

The present director of the Secret Service, Kimberly Cheatle, is a woman appointed by the Biden administration. Her priority is to make the Secret Service 30% women by 2030. This kind of Leftist thinking has invaded all of American institutions. I have written how Diversity has devastated the American military.

現在のシークレットサービスの長官、キンバリー・チートル氏はバイデン政権によって任命された女性です。彼女の優先事項は、2030年までにシークレットサービスの30パーセントを女性にすることです。この種の左翼思想はアメリカのあらゆる機関に浸透しており、多様性がいかにしてアメリカ軍を荒廃させたかについて私は書いたことがあります。

In this case, I suspect that training would focus more on eliminating prejudice against women rather than protecting a President or Presidential candidate. This is reflected in the incompetent performance of the Secret Service.

この場合、訓練は大統領や大統領候補を守ることよりも、女性に対する偏見をなくすことに重点が置かれるだろうと私は推測します。これはシークレットサービスの無能なパフォーマンスに表れています。

Or perhaps it was planned that way. There were so many mistakes made, many on the Right believe the shooter was allowed to enter, and take shots at the former President. This kind of thinking can quickly lead to a religious civil war.

Chapter 2　The American future

　あるいは、そのように計画されていたのかもしれません。あまりにも多くのミスがあったため、右派の多くは、銃撃犯が現場に入って、前大統領を狙撃することが容認されていたと信じています。このような考え方は、すぐに宗教的な内戦に発展しかねません。

When the attempt was made in 1981 on President Ronald Reagan, the response was much more professional.

　1981年にロナルド・レーガン大統領が狙われた際には、はるかにプロフェッショナルな対応がなされました。

Also, Rhetoric by prominent Democratic politicians, Hollywood celebrities and such Left-wing famous people have created a poisonous atmosphere in America. They call Trump Hitler, saying Trump should have a Bullseye put on him. Average Left-wing Americans are furious that he was not killed.

　また、著名な民主党政治家、ハリウッドセレブ、そしてそのような左翼の有名人による発言は、アメリカに有害な雰囲気を作り出しています。トランプ氏をヒトラーと呼び、トランプ氏は射撃の的にされるべきだと発言しています。平均的な左翼のアメリカ人は、トランプ氏が殺されなかったことに憤慨しています。

The religious Right is sure to see this as a miracle, and Trump standing defiantly and raising his fist is sure to set the American religious Right aflame.

第2章　アメリカの未来

　宗教右派はこれを奇跡と見なすに違いありません。そして、トランプ氏が力強く立ち上がり、こぶしを振り上げる姿は、アメリカの宗教右派を熱狂させるに違いありません。

At the rally where Trump appeared, there was a giant American flag. You can see it in the photo where he raises his fist after being shot. Apparently, just before the former President began speaking, the wind had twisted the flag into the shape of a guardian angel.

　トランプ氏が登場した集会には巨大なアメリカ国旗が掲げられていました。銃撃された後に拳を振り上げている写真にもそれが写っています。どうやら、トランプ氏が演説を始める直前に、風が国旗

Trump raises his fist under the Stars and Stripes after the shooting

銃撃後、星条旗の下で拳を突き上げるトランプ氏

Chapter 2 The American future

を守護天使の形に曲げてしまったようです。

American flag bent in the shape of a guardian angel

守護天使の形に曲がった
アメリカ国旗

https://www.parapolitika.gr/diethni/
article/1425008/donald-trab-hamos-sto-
diadiktuo-me-ton-aggelo-pou-tou-esose-ti-
zoi-to-viral-video-me-tin-amerikaniki-
simaia/

Americans on the religious Right will take this very seriously. They believe that it is a sign from God that he wishes Trump to become President and cleanse America of sin.

宗教右派のアメリカ人はこれを非常に重く受け止めるでしょう。彼らは、トランプ氏が大統領に就任し、アメリカの罪を清めることを望む神の意思であると信じています。

The civil conflict that exists in America is now taking a very serious religious turn, and that could be very violent. Well, the Left, with all its public exhibition of Drag Queens, exhibitions of statues of Satan in State Capitol buildings at Christmas, they deliberately courted such a Right wing conservative reaction.

アメリカで起きている内戦は、今や非常に深刻な宗教的様相を呈しており、非常に暴力的になる可能性もあります。左翼は、ドラァグクイーンの公共の場でのパフォーマンスや、クリスマスに州議会議事堂で悪魔の像を展示するなど、あらゆることをやってきました。彼らは、右翼保守派の反発を意図的に引き起こそうとしているのです。

How violent will things get? Only time will tell, but the game board is set, the pieces are in place.

どれほど激しい展開になるでしょうか？それは時が経てばわかるでしょう。しかし、ゲームの舞台は整い、駒も配置されました。

At the Republican convention, it has been announced that Donald Trump has chosen James David Vance as his Vice Presidential candidate. He is young, 39 years old, charismatic, a former United States Marine, and a Senator from Ohio.

共和党大会で、トランプ氏がジェームズ・デイビッド・ヴァンス氏を副大統領候補に選んだことが発表されました。ヴァンス氏は若く、39歳でカリスマ性があり、アメリカ元海兵隊員であり、オハイオ州の上院議員です。

Chapter 2 The American future

James David Vance
ディビッド・ヴァンス

He is much more competent than Kamala Harris of the Democrats. How will this all work out, well only God can tell. But now it is extremely likely that Donald Trump will become the next President.

　彼は民主党のカマラ・ハリス氏よりはるかに有能です。今後どうなるかは神のみぞ知ります。しかし、ドナルド・トランプ氏が次期大統領になる可能性は極めて高いです。

But America will still decline into chaos and disorder. And it is very unlikely that foreign born engineers and scientists will want to live in an America wracked by religious civil war. The future of America is grim.

　しかし、アメリカはなおも混沌と無秩序へと凋落していくでしょう。そして、外国生まれのエンジニアや科学者が、宗教的な内戦に苦しむアメリカに住みたいと思う可能性は非常に低いでしょう。アメリカの未来は暗いです。

第 2 章　アメリカの未来

Biden retires from the race for President

バイデン大統領選から撤退

Biden had denied he would step down from the Presidential race, despite his disastrous debate performance in June. For years, the Biden administration appears to have been run by his Chief of Staff, Jeff Zients, and his wife. Since the disastrous debate in June, his son Hunter has taken to sitting in on classified government meetings.

　バイデン氏は6月の討論会で惨敗したにもかかわらず、大統領選から撤退するつもりはないと否定しました。バイデン政権は長年、首席補佐官のジェフ・ジエンツ氏とその妻によって運営されてきたようです。惨敗した6月の討論会以来、息子ハンター氏は機密の政府会議に同席するようになりました。

Joe Biden

(46th President of the United States)

ジョー・バイデン
（第46代アメリカ合衆国大統領）

In July 2024, after suffering a near stroke while on a campaign event in Las Vegas, President Biden dropped out of the Presidential race. He was pressured by Nancy Pelosi and Barack Obama. For months, his wife had resisted pressure for him to step down; she wished to continue her

Chapter 2 The American future

lavish lifestyle as the First Lady.

　2024年7月、ラスベガスでの選挙活動中に脳卒中になりそうになった後、バイデン大統領は大統領選から撤退しました。彼はナンシー・ペロシ氏とバラク・オバマ氏から圧力を受けていました。彼の妻は数カ月間、彼に辞任を求める圧力に抵抗し、ファーストレディとして贅沢な生活を続けたいと望んでいました。

Jill Biden

(First Lady of the United States)

ジル・バイデン
（アメリカ合衆国のファーストレディ）

She appeared on the cover of Vogue magazine this summer in a $5,000 suit. After the disastrous Biden and Trump debate in June, the American media turned on Joe Biden, and attacked him and his wife. For some weeks, the American media portrayed her as the most evil woman in America, supporting her physically weak husband to satisfy her own selfish desires.

　彼女はこの夏、5000ドルのスーツを着てヴォーグ誌の表紙に登場しました。6月の悲惨なバイデン対トランプ討論会の後、アメリカのメディアはバイデン氏に背を向け、彼と彼の妻を攻撃しました。数週間にわたり、アメリカのメディアは彼女を、自分の利己的な欲

第 2 章　アメリカの未来

望を満たすために身体の弱い夫を支えるアメリカで最も邪悪な女性として描写しました。

But finally, the President gave in, and dropped out in a rather bizarre way, not announcing it in a press conference, but announcing it on X, the former Twitter. There was some speculation as to whether the announcement actually came from the President, but about a week later, he made it official in a press conference.

　しかし、最終的に大統領は屈服し、記者会見ではなく、X（元ツイッター）で発表するというかなり奇妙な方法で辞退しました。この発表が本当に大統領からのものだったのかどうかについては憶測が飛び交いましたが、約1週間後、彼は記者会見で公式に発表しました。

As a requirement of his departure, he endorsed Vice President Kamala Harris as the next Presidential candidate. Again, this was extremely irregular, there was no Democratic Party vote. She was simply picked by the party leaders. Perhaps it was Biden's revenge upon the Democratic Party for having kicked him out.

　辞任の条件として、彼は次期大統領候補としてカマラ・ハリス副大統領を推薦しました。これもまた非常に異例なことで、民主党の投票はありませんでした。彼女は単に党首によって選ばれただけです。おそらくこれは、バイデン氏が自分を追い出した民主党に対する復讐だったのでしょう。

The United States government has become a farce. So President Biden has become a "lame duck" President, or one with little influence and power. Actually, he is just about the worst American President ever.

アメリカ政府は茶番劇と化しました。バイデン大統領は「レームダック」大統領、つまり影響力と権力のほとんどない大統領となりました。実際、彼はアメリカ史上最悪の大統領です。

Kamala Harris & Tim Walz
カマラ・ハリスとティム・ウォルツ

She was chosen for Vice President because she is a non-white woman. Her English language is often incomprehensible. In polls putting her or Joe Biden against Donald Trump in an election, she fares much worse.

彼女が副大統領に選ばれたのは、彼女が白人女性ではないからです。彼女の英語はしばしば理解不能です。選挙で彼女またはバイデン氏とトランプ氏を比較した世論調査では、彼女の成績ははるかに悪いです。

She is not at all popular with any traditional Democratic groups, including Black people. Recently, Donald Trump held a rally in the state of Michigan where he was popular throughout the state including the heavily Black city of Detroit.

彼女は黒人を含む伝統的な民主党グループから全く人気がありま

せん。最近、トランプ氏はミシガン州で集会を開き、黒人の多い都市デトロイトを含む州全体で人気がありました。

Many Blacks and Hispanics, traditionally Democrat, have moved towards Donald Trump. Inflation is very high in America, many Americans cannot afford to eat and depend on charities for food.

伝統的に民主党支持だった黒人やヒスパニック系の多くは、トランプ氏に傾倒しています。アメリカではインフレが非常に深刻で、多くのアメリカ人は食事をする余裕がなく、食料を慈善団体に頼っています。

Kamala Harris
カマラ・ハリス

The policies of Kamala Harris as a possible President will probably be even more Left-wing than Joe Biden. Even though she has no accomplishments in her public life, her father is a Marxist professor at Stanford University. We do know she favors defunding police forces.

次期大統領候補のカマラ・ハリス氏の政策は、おそらくバイデン大統領よりもさらに左翼的でしょう。彼女は公職で何の実績もあり

Chapter 2 The American future

ませんが、父親はスタンフォード大学の教授でマルクス主義者です。彼女が警察予算の削減を支持していることはわかっています。

With former President Obama finally announcing his support, she appears to have been chosen as the nominee.

　オバマ元大統領がついに支持を表明したため、彼女が候補者に選ばれたようです。

Throughout the three and a half years of the Biden administration, Kamala Harris has proven to be extremely unpopular, and after being given the job of addressing the problems of the migrant crisis on the southern border, she made no effort and completely failed.

　バイデン政権の3年半を通じて、ハリス氏は極めて不人気であることが証明され、南部国境の移民危機の問題に取り組む任務を与えられながらも、何の努力もせず、完全に失敗しました。

President Biden has Alzheimer's and can no longer make intelligent speeches, but he used to be a Senator, and functioned in that capacity. Kamala Harris had risen quickly to Senator from California.

　バイデン大統領はアルツハイマー病を患っており、もはや知的な演説はできませんが、かつては上院議員であり、その職務を果たしていました。ハリス氏はカリフォルニア州の上院議員に急速に上り詰めました。

The Democrats dare not allow Kamala Harris to speak in front of a camera without a set script. In the 2020 election, her support never exceeded 2% of the people. The only people who support her now are transgenders, and they are a tiny minority.

民主党はハリス氏が決まった台本なしでカメラの前で話すことを決して許しません。2020年の選挙では、彼女への支持は国民の2%を超えることはありませんでした。現在彼女を支持しているのはトランスジェンダーの人々だけであり、彼らはごく少数派です。

It is certain that the Democrats will cheat in the election. Mail-in ballots will be used, illegal immigrants will vote, even if they have no right to do so. But now, the question arises: will it be enough?

民主党が選挙で不正を働くことは確実です。郵便投票が使われるでしょうし、不法移民も投票する権利がないにもかかわらず投票するでしょう。しかし、ここで疑問が湧きます。それで十分なのでしょうか?

Myself, I am very concerned about the prospect of Kamala Harris as President. Living as I do in Japan, I wonder how this will affect America's reputation on the international scene. President Biden did a lot of damage to America as a senile President.

私自身、ハリス氏が大統領になる可能性について非常に懸念しています。日本に住んでいる私としては、これが国際舞台でのアメリカの評判にどのような影響を与えるのか気になります。バイデン大

Chapter 2 The American future

統領は老齢の大統領としてアメリカに多大な損害を与えました。

But he had at least been a serious and intelligent politician for many years. Kamala Harris has nothing, despite media efforts to portray her in a good light.

 しかし、少なくとも彼は長年、真面目で知的な政治家でした。ハリス氏には何もないので、メディアが彼女を良い印象で描こうと努力しています。

She has very little actual political history, and her policies tend to be very Marxist. As her running mate, she has chosen Tim Walz, Governor of Minnesota. He is another radical leftist, a supporter of LGBT, for example, supporting children having sex change operations at a young age, even against the wishes of their parents.

 彼女には実際の政治経験がほとんどなく、彼女の政策はマルクス主義的傾向が強いです。彼女は副大統領候補としてミネソタ州のティム・ウォルツ知事を選びました。彼もまた過激な左翼で、LGBTの支持者であり、例えば親の意に反して幼い子供が性転換手術を受けることなどを支持しています。

Also he has a major scandal in his military career. He was a non-commissioned officer in the Minnesota National Guard. The National Guard functions as an Army Reserve. The units remain in their home state, but they can be called to active duty to serve overseas.

第2章　アメリカの未来

　また、彼は軍人としての経歴において大きなスキャンダルを抱えています。彼はミネソタ州の州兵で下士官でした。州兵は予備役として機能しています。部隊はそれぞれの州に駐留していますが、海外での任務に就くために招集されることもあります。

Tim Walz
ティム・ウォルツ

Tim Walz's unit was called up to go to Iraq, and he then quit. However, in speeches, he has claimed he served in wartime military service. For Americans, military service is a very sensitive issue, and making false claims is not looked upon well.

　ウォルツ氏の部隊はイラク派遣のため招集されましたが、その後彼は退役しました。しかし、演説の中で彼は戦時中兵役に就いていたと主張しています。アメリカ人にとって兵役は非常にデリケートな問題であり、虚偽の主張をすることは好ましくありません。

His extreme Leftism and his murky military service could be serious problems for the Democratic Party in the general election. But the Democrats have a plan to win the election. They will simply give voting rights to the over ten million illegal migrants that who entered America under the Biden administration.

　彼の極左思想と不透明な軍歴は、総選挙で民主党にとって深刻な問題となる可能性があります。しかし、民主党には選挙に勝つための計画があります。彼らは、バイデン政権下でアメリカに入国した1000万人以上の不法移民に投票権を与えるというものです。

These people are currently being provided with food and lodging courtesy of local municipalities, which is causing them to go bankrupt. Actual Americans are being forced out of their living places to make room for illegal migrants.

　これらの人々は、地方自治体の厚意により食料と宿泊場所を提供されて暮らしていますが、それが財政破綻の原因となっています。不法移民の住居が優先され、そのために生活に困窮するアメリカ人が住居を失っているのです。

The Democrats seem to feel these people will vote for the Democrats out of gratitude. Well to me, this seems to be a very risky policy. Will it work in the election? We can only wait and see.

　民主党は、これらの人々が感謝の気持ちから民主党に投票するだろうと考えているようです。私にとって、これは非常に不安定な政策のように思えます。選挙でうまくいくでしょうか？　待って見守るしかありません。

第 2 章 アメリカの未来

And Kamala Harris and Tim Walz have yet to participate in a press conference, or to outline their policies in any detail. How will this unford? Again, time will tell.

ハリス氏とウォルツ氏はまだ記者会見に参加しておらず、政策の詳細も明らかにしていません。どうなるでしょうか？これもまた、時が経てばわかるでしょう。

Robert Kennedy Junior endorses Trump
ロバート・ケネディ・ジュニア、トランプ支持を表明

And now, in late August, a bombshell dropped from the Republicans. Robert Kennedy Junior has endorsed Donald Trump for President. He will continue his independent campaign in blue states, but campaign for Trump in swing states.

そして今、8月下旬、共和党から衝撃のニュースが飛び出しました。ロバート・ケネディ・ジュニア氏がドナルド・トランプ氏を大統領候補として支持しました。彼は民主党支持の州では無所属の選挙活動を続けますが、激戦州ではトランプを支持するつもりです。

This is a very serious blow to the Democrats. It has been over a month since Kamala Harris was declared to be the Democratic Presidential candidate. There was no primary election, simply top Democrats picked her as the candidate. She has made no campaign speeches, other than spouting very socialist-type economic policies, which have historically failed.

Chapter 2 The American future

　これは民主党にとって非常に深刻な打撃です。ハリス氏が民主党の大統領候補であると宣言してから1カ月以上が経ちました。予備選挙はなく、単に民主党のトップが彼女を候補に選んだだけです。彼女は選挙演説で、うまくいったためしがない極めて社会主義的な経済政策を唱える以外には、何もしていません。

Trump and Kennedy, along with J. D. Vance as the Vice Presidential candidate, make a formidable team.

　トランプ氏とケネディ氏、そして副大統領候補のJ・D・ヴァンス氏は、強力なチームを形成します。

Robert Kennedy Junior used to be a Democrat. If the Democratic party had let him become the candidate, he would have been a very capable opponent to Donald Trump. But top Democrats insisted on someone they could control so they kept Joe Biden as the candidate.

　ケネディ氏はかつて民主党員でした。もし民主党が彼を候補者にしていたなら、彼はトランプ氏の非常に有能な対抗馬になっていたでしょう。しかし、民主党幹部は自分たちがコントロールできる人物を主張し、バイデン氏を候補者に据えました。

They demonized Kennedy, using murky legal actions to remove him from state ballots as an independent. So he got angry, and has joined Trump.

そして彼らはケネディ氏を悪者にし、曖昧な法的手段を使って彼を無所属候補として州の投票から排除しました。それで彼は怒り、トランプ氏に同調しました。

It will be an exciting few months until the election.

選挙まであと数カ月は楽しみな時期となるでしょう。

The elections, how will they go?
2024 大統領選の見通し

So this is who the Democrats put forth in Kamala Harris to battle Donald Trump for the Presidency. Do they really expect her to do well? Well, the Left lives in a world of fantasy. After all, they believe that a man can change into a woman, and vice versa.

民主党は、トランプ氏と大統領選を戦うために、ハリス氏を擁立しました。本当に彼女がうまくいくと期待しているのでしょうか？ まあ、左派は空想の世界に生きています。結局のところ、彼らは男性が女性に変身できると信じているし、その逆もまた同じです。

Average people on the Left still express extreme hate for Donald Trump. They publicly say that they regret that the shooter missed. The population is about evenly split.

そして、左派の平均的な人々は、依然としてトランプ氏に対して

激しい憎悪を表明しています。彼らは、銃撃犯が外したことを残念に思うと公に述べています。人口はほぼ均等に分かれています。

I do not believe that the Democrats can win in any kind of fair election. So what will they do? Give up and let Kamala Harris humiliate herself? Or will they try some kind of massive act of cheating, like another pandemic, with mail-in ballots? We can only wait and see.

　民主党がいかなる公正な選挙でも勝てるとは思えません。では彼らはどうするでしょうか？諦めてハリス氏に恥をかかせるのか？それとも、またパンデミックのようなものを起こし、郵便投票による大規模な不正行為を試みるのか？　私たちはただ待って見守るしかありません。

Donald Trump's survival of the assassination attempt on July 13th has really energized the Christian Fundamentalists. For them, all this emphasis on Drag Queens and sexual perversity is against God. If the Democrats cheat and Kamala Harris wins, I expect violence from them in 2025.

　トランプ氏が7月13日の暗殺未遂事件を生き延びたことで、キリスト教原理主義者（福音派）たちは大いに元気づけられました。彼らにとって、ドラァグクイーンや性的倒錯をこれほど強調することは神への冒涜です。もし民主党が不正をしてハリス氏が勝利すれば、2025年に彼らが暴動を起こすと予想します。

For the Left, they love to insult traditional culture and Christianity. I understand the opening performance of the Paris Olympics featured a Drag Queen show of Jesus's last supper. This kind of thing is just trouble. If Trump wins the election, which is now highly probable, the Left will likely riot in 2025.

　左翼は伝統文化やキリスト教を侮辱するのが大好きです。パリ五輪の開会式では、イエスの最後の晩餐を演じるドラァグクイーンのショーが行われたと聞いています。このようなことはただ厄介なだけです。トランプ氏が選挙に勝てば（今やその可能性は高い）、左翼は2025年に暴動を起こす可能性が高いです。

It will be a very difficult time for America, and for countries like Japan, which are so intertwined with America.

　アメリカにとって、そしてアメリカと深く結びついている日本のような国々にとって、非常に困難な時期となるでしょう。

Chapter 3 What should Japan do?
第3章 日本は何をすべきか？

First and formost, what not to do.
まず第一に、してはいけないこと

This is how I will begin this section: what not to do. Do not behave like former Prime Minister Kishida. He is obsessed with being accepted on equal term by foreigners. I really did not enjoy seeing the photos of him hosting the G7 event, or attending it in Italy, he looked like an overly eager young boy.

　このセクションでは、まずしてはいけないことについて述べようと思います。岸田前首相のような振舞いはしないでください。彼は外国人から対等に扱われることに夢中になっています。彼がG7イベントを主催したり、イタリアサミットに参加している写真を見るのは耐え難いものでした。彼は気負いすぎた少年のように見えました。

And he has a very unhealthy relationship with the present American ambassador Rahm Emanuel. Kishida seems to rely on Emanuel for advice on how to govern Japan. Mr. Emanuel is merely an ambassador, Mr. Kishida is the leader of Japan.

　そして彼は現アメリカ大使ラーム・エマニュエル氏と非常に不健全な関係にあります。岸田首相は、日本をどのように統治するのかについて、彼に助言を求めているようです。エマニュエル氏は単な

る大使であり、岸田氏は日本のリーダーです。

Prime Minister Kishida seems eager to give Japanese money to foreigners, particularly Ukraine. That country is the most corrupt in Europe, 70% of supplies sent never make it to front line; they disappear into pockets of numerous officials, and are resold on the Black Market.

　岸田首相は、日本の資金を外国、特にウクライナに投入することに熱心なようです。ウクライナはヨーロッパで最も腐敗した国で、送られた物資の70パーセントは前線に届かず、闇市場で転売され、多くの役人の懐に消えています。

While Japan is in trouble, such as the Noto earthquake and the weak yen, he simply gives money to foreigners. They do not accept him or respect him, they despise him. If Japan is in trouble, no other country will come to our aid.

　日本が能登半島地震や円安など、様々な問題を抱えているときに、彼はただ外国人にお金をばら撒いています。彼らは岸田首相を受け入れず、尊敬もせず、軽蔑しています。日本が困っているとき、彼らは日本を助けに来ないでしょう。

There are so many Japanese who seem to be this way.

　こういう日本人はたくさんいるようです。

Chapter 3 What should Japan do?

I call it the "Black Ship Complex". When Commodore Perry first arrived with his fleet of Black Ships in 1853, he had steam powered warships which did not depend on the wind for movement, which shocked Japan, which had long been isolated.

　私はこれを「黒船コンプレックス」と呼んでいます。1853年にペリー提督が初めて日本に来航したとき、風力に頼らない蒸気動力の黒船艦隊を率いていました。これは、長い間鎖国していた日本に衝撃を与えました。

Also, defeat in the Second World war convinced many Japanese of the superiority of foreigners, particularly Americans. After that war, the American government had an active propaganda operation, the War Guilt Information Program, to convince Japanese people that they had done evil things in the war. Of course, this was not at all true.

　また、第二次世界大戦での敗北は、多くの日本人に外国人、特にアメリカ人の優越性を確信させました。その戦争の後、アメリカ政府はウォー・ギルト・インフォメーション・プログラム（戦争犯罪広報計画）という積極的なプロパガンダ活動を展開し、日本人に戦争で悪いことをしたと信じ込ませようとしました。もちろん、これは全く真実ではありませんでした。

But many people believed it, and actually worshipped America. For a time, I think such American worship was necessary. America would have been much crueler towards Japan otherwise.

しかし、多くの人々がそれを信じ、そしてアメリカを崇拝しました。一時期、そのようなアメリカ崇拝は必要だったのだと思います。そうでなければ、アメリカは日本に対してもっと残酷な扱いをしたでしょう。

But now, the attitude of Prime Minister Kishida towards foreigners, funding them, introducing their legal concepts into Japan, such as the LGBT law, is becoming harmful to Japan.

しかし、今の岸田首相の外国人に対する態度（彼らに資金を提供したり、LGBT法のような彼らの法概念を日本に導入すること）は、日本を危険な方向へと向かわせています。

Since the first contact with the West, Japan has always produced superior systems. In the Second World War, Japanese ships and aircraft were superior. The problem was that America could produce more.

日本は西洋との最初の接触以来、常に優れたシステムを生み出してきました。第二次世界大戦では、日本の船舶や航空機は優れていました。問題は、アメリカの方が大量に生産できたことです。

In the Tokugawa Shogunate, Japan produced the most just and advanced system of government in the world. Japan had the cleanest cities, the healthiest population. When Perry came to Japan, American and European cities were filthy and disease-ridden.

徳川幕府の時代、日本は世界で最も公正で先進的な政治体制を築

Chapter 3 What should Japan do?

き上げました。日本の都市は最も清潔で、国民は最も健康でした。ペリーが日本に来たとき、アメリカやヨーロッパの都市は不潔で病気が蔓延していました。

This is because Japanese people excel in organization. The existence of Tokugawa society threatened Americans. When Perry came to Japan, only 40% of Americans were literate in the English language with 26 letters.

これは日本人が組織力に優れているからです。徳川社会の存在はアメリカ人にとって脅威でした。ペリーが日本に来た当時、26文字の英語を読解できたのはアメリカ人の40パーセントでした。

In Japan, however the Japanese language consists of three writing systems, Chinese ideographs(kanji), and the alphabets of hiragana and katakana. 80% of Japanese people could read those. This shocked Americans.

日本では、日本語には漢字とひらがな、カタカナの3種の文字体系があります。日本人の80パーセントがそれらを読むことができました。これはアメリカ人に衝撃を与えました。

Now, when a Japanese person is shocked in some way, they will work harder to overcome whatever difficulty exists they face. An American, or most Westerners, in contrast will try to destroy the object causing the shock — in this case the Japanese writing system.

第3章　日本は何をすべきか？

　日本人は何らかの衝撃を受けると、どんな困難があってもそれを克服するために一層努力します。アメリカ人、そしてほとんどの西洋人は、その衝撃を与えた対象、この場合は日本語の文字体系を破壊しようとします。

That is why, during the Meiji era and again after the Second World War, there were effort to have Japan adopt a Romanized alphabet. Personally, I do not believe American literacy rates have improved much since Commodore Perry's time, American schools are that bad.

　そのため、明治時代や第二次世界大戦後、日本でローマ字表記を採用させようという動きがありました。個人的には、アメリカの識字率はペリー提督の時代と比べてそれほど向上していないと思います。アメリカの学校はそれほどひどいのです。

However, I am shocked at how awful Japanese schools are when it comes to historical education. They seem to teach that Japan, after the Meiji Restoration embarked on a path of conquest.

　しかし、歴史教育に関して日本の学校がどれほどひどいものか、私は衝撃を受けています。明治維新後の日本は侵略の道を歩み始めたと教えられているようです。

The truth is that Spain, France, Great Britain and the United States were predatory colonialists. Also Portugal. So it is no accident that America pushes this line. The Americans truly believe that Japan was an evil nation until America brought Democracy.

Chapter 3 What should Japan do?

　真実は、スペイン、フランス、イギリス、そしてアメリカが強欲な植民地主義者だったということです。ポルトガルもです。ですから、アメリカが日本を悪魔化する主張を推し進めるのは偶然ではありません。アメリカ人は、アメリカが民主主義をもたらすまで日本は邪悪な国だったと本気で信じています。

Actually, Japan's overseas acquisitions in Korea and Taiwan were not colonial in nature, but annexations. The lives of citizens in those areas were brought to the level of Japan proper, with equality. This was something that the Imperial European powers, including America, did not do. They kept the local populations of their colonies subservient.

　実際、日本が海外に獲得した朝鮮と台湾は、植民地にしたのではなく併合でした。これらの地域の住民の生活は、日本本土と同等のレベルにまで高められ、平等に扱われました。これは、アメリカを含むヨーロッパ帝国主義列強が決して行わなかったことです。彼らは植民地の住民を隷属させ続けました。

And Japan established its own Democracy in 1868 with the creation of a Parliament. Americans always say that this was actually a dictatorship, but frankly, given the current political and social mess in America, they should remain quiet out of shame.

　そして日本は1868年に議会を創設し、独自の民主主義を確立しました。アメリカ人は、これは実際には独裁政治だったと言っていますが、率直に言って、今のアメリカの政治的、社会的混乱を見れば、彼らはそれを恥じて黙っているべきでしょう。

But this teaching that the Japanese were an awful nation until reformed by Americans, is doing significant harm to the Japanese people. It is a psychological harm, that affects how people feel and react.

　しかし、アメリカ人によって改革されるまで日本はひどい国だったという教育は、日本人に悪影響を及ぼしています。それは日本人の精神に傷を負わせ、人々の意識や行動に悪い影響を与えます。

It is difficult to expect the Japanese government to act in this manner. They are proving incapable of serious action. We should establish our own system of schools for young people, like juku. And create our own textbooks.

　日本政府にその対処を期待するのは難しいです。日本政府には行動する能力がないことが証明されています。私たちは、私塾のような形の、若者のための独自の学校制度を確立すべきです。そして、独自の教科書を作成するべきです。

This is one place where people can concentrate their energy for good positive outcomes. A truly grassroots action, for the young people of Japan.

　ここは、人々が素晴らしい成果を出すために力を結集できる場所の一つです。日本の若者たちを主体とした、まさに草の根的な活動です。

However, what other actions should Japan take, with the dramatic

Chapter 3 What should Japan do?

decline of America?

しかし、アメリカが劇的に衰退する中で、日本は他にどのような行動を取るべきなのでしょうか？

The expansion of the Japanese military
日本軍を増強せよ

First, let us look at the military.

まず、軍隊について見てみましょう。

The Navy. We should double the number of surface warships to around 100. Surface warships are aircraft carriers, cruisers, and destroyers. However, submarines will be very important, 60 would be ideal. this would allow 20 to be at sea at all times. In the military, there is a rule of three. With 60 submarines, 20 will be at sea on patrol, 20 will be returning to port, and 20 will be leaving port to go on patrol.

海軍は水上艦艇の数を倍増して約100隻に増やすべきです。水上艦艇は航空母艦、巡洋艦、駆逐艦です。しかし、潜水艦は非常に重要で、60隻あれば最適です。これにより、常に20隻が海上にいられることになります。軍隊には3つのルールがあります。60隻の潜水艦のうち、20隻は海上で哨戒し、20隻は港に戻り、20隻は港を出て哨戒に向かいます。

Present day Japanese submarines and torpedoes are the best in the world.

　現在の日本の潜水艦と魚雷は世界最高です。

Air Force fighters should be doubled to around 558.

　空軍の戦闘機は倍増の 558 機程度にすべきです。

The Army should be increased to around 450,000 troops. However, a large part of these can be Reserves, and in normal times work at civilian jobs. The same can be said for ships and aircraft; some can be kept in Reserve, and activated in times of emergency.

　陸軍は 45 万人程度に増強すべきです。ただし、その大部分は予備役として、平時は民間の仕事に従事します。海軍、空軍も同様であり、緊急時に備えて予備役を確保しておきます。

Some people will say that Japanese are not capable of this, as they are spiritually weak. No, not at all. I was a United States Marine. I sometimes meet young Japanese people when I go out drinking. They will do fine in military units.

　日本人は精神的に弱く、軍人には向かないと言う人もいるでしょう。いいえ、そんなことはありません。私はアメリカ海兵隊員でした。飲みに行くと時々日本の若者に会います。彼らは立派にやっていけるでしょう。

Chapter 3 What should Japan do?

What they need is proper training and leadership. And they need a sense of pride in their nation and themselves. This Left-wing masochistic education is designed to destroy people. Much of it is done by foreigners, in particular Koreans.

　彼らに必要なのは、適切な訓練と正しい指導です。そして、彼らは自分たちの国と自分自身に誇りを持つ必要があります。この左翼的でマゾヒスティックな教育は、人々を破滅させるために作られています。その多くは、特に韓国人などの外国人によって引き起こされています。

In Korea, most of the historical protests are done by leftists, I have written a book about the things that Japan did during the annexation period.

　韓国では、過去の歴史に関する抗議活動のほとんどは左翼によって行われていますが、私は日本が併合期に行ったことについて本を書きました(『アメリカ人が語るアメリカが隠しておきたい日本の歴史』)。

I believe Koreans are actually jealous of Japan.

　実際、韓国人は日本に嫉妬していると思います。

Many Left-wing Japanese think that war will happen because Japan has a military. Not at all. The opposite is true. Any country will attack a weak country, but no one nobody will attack a strong country.

多くの日本の左翼は、日本に軍隊があるから戦争が起こると考えています。全く違います。真実はその逆です。どんな国も弱い国を攻撃し、強い国を攻撃することはありません。

We must also create an intelligence service both foreign and domestic.

我々は国内外を対象とした諜報機関も創設する必要があります。

But in any case Japan should build up a system of national service in fields like the military, farming, fishing, elderly care.

しかしいずれにせよ、日本は国民奉仕制度を構築すべきです。軍事、農業、漁業、高齢者介護などの分野においてです。

When people graduate from high school or university, they should spend a few years in the military, or farming, or elderly care. This would also build pride and character and reduce the number of youth with emotional and mental problems.

高校や大学を卒業したら、軍隊や農業、老人介護などで数年間を過ごすべきです。そうすることで自尊心と人格が育まれ、情緒的、精神的問題を抱える若者が減るでしょう。

We should propose to America that Japan become the "Shield of Democracy" While America faces internal troubles, we will increase our military strength in Asia and defend shared values.

Chapter 3 What should Japan do?

　アメリカに対して、日本が「民主主義の盾」となることを提案すべきです。アメリカが国内問題を抱えている間、私たちはアジアで軍事力を強化し、共通の価値観を守ります。

In the past, the Japanese relied on America to defend itself, but now things are reversed; America will have to rely on Japan to defend shared interests in Asia.

　過去、日本は日本を守るためにアメリカに頼っていましたが、今では状況は逆転し、アメリカはアジアにおける共通の利益を守るために日本に頼らざるを得なくなります。

At first, the Americans will probably insist on having an American commander, but after about 10 years, we could have a Japanese commander.

　最初は、アメリカ人はアメリカ人の司令官を主張するでしょうが、10年後くらいには日本人の司令官が就任する可能性もあります。

We must also surround the American commanders with Japanese staff so that they do not provoke any reckless military adventures in Asia.

　また、アメリカ軍司令官らがアジアで無謀な軍事冒険を起こさないように、彼らを日本人スタッフで取り囲まなければなりません。

Gradually, America will be forced to withdraw troops to fulfill duties inside the United States, and eventually the American military garrison in Japan may be eliminated. Japan will be responsible for the defending Asia.

徐々に、アメリカはアメリカ国内での任務のために軍隊を撤退させざるを得なくなり、最終的には日本に駐留する米軍部隊も撤収することになるでしょう。日本はアジアの防衛に責任を持つことになるでしょう。

Foreigners in Japan
日本に住む外国人

We do not need foreigners in Japan at all. We must make better use of Japanese workers. This will mean that some companies will lose profits. That is unfortunate. The entire system of bringing foreign workers into Japan for vocational training must be abolished.

日本に外国人はまったく必要ありません。日本人をもっと活用すべきです。そうすると利益を出せなくなる会社も出てきます。それは残念なことです。しかし、外国人を日本が受け入れて職業訓練を行うという制度は全面的に廃止すべきです。

Groups like the Vietnamese should be helped to return to Vietnam. The end of this insane refugee program for Kurds is a good way to reduce their population. Already, the Kurds are talking on social media about declaring their own nation in Kawaguchi city in Saitama.

Chapter 3 What should Japan do?

　ベトナム人のようなグループはベトナムに帰国できるよう支援すべきです。非常識な難民プログラムを終わらせることは、クルド人の人口を減らす良い方法です。すでにクルド人は埼玉県川口市を自分たちの国家として宣言することをソーシャルメディア上で話しています。

Eventually, this will evolve from a police problem to a problem that requires the intervention of the Japanese Army, and that will be bloody.

　最終的に、これは警察が扱う問題から軍隊の介入を要する問題へと発展し、流血の事態となるでしょう。

Left-wing politicians will scream that Japan needs to be more diverse, no we do not. Foreigners who do come here should be required to speak Japanese and obey Japanese laws and cultural norms.

　左翼の政治家は日本はもっと多様性が必要だと叫ぶでしょうが、必要ありません。日本に来る外国人は日本語を話し、日本の法律や慣習に従うべきです。

Please look at America, it is being destroyed by diversity initiatives. A country needs one language and one culture.

　アメリカを見てください。多様性推進政策によってアメリカは破壊されつつあります。国家には一つの言語、一つの文化が必要です。

To live in Japan is a privilege, not a right. There will be a problem with American refugees though. Over the years, many Americans and Japanese have intermarried.

　日本に住むことは権利ではなく特権です。しかし、アメリカ人難民が生じた場合、問題が起きるでしょう。長年にわたり、アメリカ人と日本人の間で多くの国際結婚がありました。

They will have a legal right to residence in Japan. As America faces collapse, many of these people will come to live in Japan. However, if the husband is American, it is highly unlikely that he will speak any reasonable level of Japanese. Furthermore this person will certainly know nothing about the Japanese work environment.

　彼らは日本に居住する権利が法的に認められます。アメリカが崩壊すると、これらの人々の多くが日本に移住してくるでしょう。しかし、夫がアメリカ人の場合、ある程度の日本語を話せる可能性は極めて低いでしょう。また、このような人は日本の労働環境について何も知りません。

These people should be helped to begin again in Japan in the farming and fishing industries. These are occupations where they can learn by observing. Many people will complain that in America they were lawyers or architects, but they will not be able to continue that profession in Japan.

　これらの人々は日本で農業や漁業に就労して再出発できるよう支

Chapter 3 What should Japan do?

援を受けるべきです。これらは実践しながら学べる職業です。アメリカでは弁護士や建築家だったのに、日本ではその職業に就けないなどと不満を言う人がたくさん出てくるでしょう。

This program of introducing people to farming will also be useful for Japanese people who lose their jobs because the collapse of American.

　農業への参入プログラムは、アメリカの崩壊で職を失った日本人にとっても有益なものとなるでしょう。

Japanese people still do not understand what I mean when I say the collapse of American. The Japanese media does not report any negative news at all about America.

　日本の人々は、私が言う「アメリカの崩壊」の意味をまだよく理解していません。日本のメディアは、アメリカに関するネガティブなニュースを全く報道しません。

Yet through social media, Japanese people have begun to realize that America is in deep trouble, with many problems and festering civil conflict. In this book, I have tried to clarify this.

　しかし、ソーシャルメディアを通じて、アメリカが多くの問題を抱え、深刻な内紛状態に陥っていることを、日本人は徐々に認識し始めています。本書では、このことを明らかにしようと試みました。

Some people say Japan should help America. No. Americans must do this themselves. America is too big; we cannot help them. In fact, we should help Japan, for example, the survivors of the Noto earthquake.

日本はアメリカを助けるべきだと言う人もいます。いいえ、アメリカ人自身がやらなければなりません。アメリカは大きすぎるので、私たちは彼らを助けることはできません。私たちは、たとえば能登半島地震の被災者など、日本を助けるべきなのです。

A new foreign policy
外交上の新しい選択肢

In foreign policy, Japan must understand that the American military will not be a partner for much longer. With all their domestic problems, they will lose the ability to act.

外交政策においては、日本はアメリカ軍がもう長くパートナーでいられないことを理解しなければなりません。国内問題を抱える中で、アメリカ軍はその能力を失うでしょう。

For the defense of Japan, the most important thing is to establish good and strong relations with Russia, and Vietnam. China has become an aggressive country in Asia, and Russian and Vietnamese alliance would help keep China in check.

日本の防衛にとって最も重要なことは、ロシア、ベトナムと良好

Chapter 3 What should Japan do?

かつ強固な関係を築くことです。中国はアジアで侵略的な国となっており、ロシアとベトナムの同盟は中国を牽制するのに役立つでしょう。

Why do I say these two countries? Throughout the centuries, Vietnam has been attacked by China some 22 times, and each time they triumphed over China.

なぜこの二つの国を挙げるのでしょうか。何世紀にもわたって、ベトナムは中国から22回ほど攻撃を受けてきましたが、そのたびに中国に勝利してきました。

Russia may surprise some people. Many Japanese would see Russia as an enemy. Well that may have been true before, but things change.

ロシアについては、驚く人もいることでしょう。多くの日本人はロシアを敵視しています。確かに以前はそうだったかもしれませんが、状況は変わるものです。

Russia today is very different from the old Soviet Union. In fact, it can be said that politically speaking, Russia is much freer than America. Things have flipped.

現在のロシアは、かつてのソ連とは大きく異なります。実際、政治的には、ロシアはアメリカよりもはるかに自由であると言えます。状況は一変したのです。

And Russia and China are not always friends. Just as recently as 2008, Russia was war gaming a war with China in Kazakhstan. It is American mistakes in Ukraine that have pushed Russia and China into an alliance. It may break apart again.

　そして、ロシアと中国は必ずしも友好関係にあるわけではありません。2008年にロシアはカザフスタンで中国との戦争を想定した軍事演習を行いました。ウクライナにおけるアメリカの過ちが、ロシアと中国を同盟関係に追い込んだのです。しかし再び関係が壊れる可能性があります。

An alliance with Vietnam in the south and Russia in the north would significantly deter Chinese aggression towards Japan. And Russia would benefit from Japanese investment in Siberia.

　南のベトナム、北のロシアとの同盟は、日本に対する中国の侵略を大いに抑止するでしょう。そしてロシアにとっても、シベリアへの日本の投資は有益なものとなります。

Russia is a very stable country both politically and socially, and will become the most powerful country in the world. America and Europe are collapsing.

　ロシアは政治的にも社会的にも非常に安定した国であり、世界で最も強力な国になるでしょう。アメリカとヨーロッパは崩壊しつつあります。

Chapter 3 What should Japan do?

Japan should not cling to what once was and is gone forever, but should embrace the new future.

　日本は、かつて存在したが今はもうないものに固執するのではなく、新しい未来を受け入れるべきです。

We should also abandon the G7 and any NATO cooperation. Europe is also in a state of collapse, they cannot help Japan in any way. The war in Ukraine is lost. They only want Japanese money. Japan is part of Asia, not Europe.

　G7やNATOとの協力も破棄すべきです。ヨーロッパも崩壊状態にあり、日本を助けることはできません。ウクライナ戦争は彼らの敗北です。彼らが欲しいのは日本の金だけです。日本はアジアの一部であり、ヨーロッパではありません。

We should also send a Japanese military garrison to Hawaii. Something like two Japanese battalions, and one Vietnamese battalion. We could say they are for training.

　ハワイにも日本軍の駐屯地を設置すべきです。派遣するのは、たとえば日本人の部隊2個大隊とベトナム人で構成された部隊1個大隊です。これらは訓練のための派遣という名目で行います。

The American military will soon lose the ability to garrison in Hawaii; troops will be needed on the mainland. We could state that the Japanese troops are for training. But this could help prevent a Chinese takeover attempt of Hawaii, and yes, they will try.

アメリカ軍はまもなくハワイに駐留できなくなります。本土に軍隊が必要になるからです。日本軍は訓練の名目で駐留できるでしょう。これは中国によるハワイ占領の試みを防ぐのに役立ちます。実際、中国はハワイの占領を試みるでしょう。

The Vietnamese battalion could be sent home to Vietnam after completing their service, and this will help keep good relations with Vietnam, which is essential.

ベトナム人の大隊は任務を終えればベトナムに帰国することもできます。これはベトナムとの良好な関係を維持する上で不可欠です。

The idea of the Vietnamese battalion is just that: an idea. It would have three purposes. One would be to remove troublesome foreigners from Japan. Another would be to improve ties with Vietnam. And the third would be to help guard Hawaii.

ベトナム大隊の構想は、あくまで構想です。その構想には3つの目的があります。1つは、問題のある外国人を日本の外に出すこと。もう1つは、ベトナムとの関係を改善すること。そして3つ目は、ハワイの警備に協力することです。

The foreign Kenshusei system, or foreign trainee system, is full of abuse. Many Vietnamese have simply been abandoned by their employers. They lack the funds to return to Vietnam.So many have

Chapter 3 What should Japan do?

turned to a life of crime in Gunma and Tochigi prefectures.

外国人研修生制度は虐待に満ちています。多くのベトナム人は雇用主に見捨てられ、ベトナムに帰国する資金がなく、群馬県や栃木県で犯罪に手を染める者も少なくありません。

To simply arrest them and deport them back to Vietnam would strain Japanese ties with Vietnam. This is a country that Japan needs to be friends with. Vietnam has military conscription, so that most Vietnamese men would have military experience.

彼らを逮捕してベトナムに強制送還するだけでは、日本とベトナムの関係にひびが入るでしょう。ベトナムは日本が友好関係を築く必要のある国です。ベトナムには兵役制度があり、ほとんどのベトナム人男性は兵役経験を持っています。

They would, of course, be paid for their service in Japanese uniform, and this would enable them to buy a house or shop upon their return to Vietnam. This would help strengthen our ties with Vietnam, and help the anti-Chinese alliance.

もちろん、彼らには日本軍の制服を着用して任務に就くことに対して報酬が支払われ、ベトナムに帰国後、家や店を持つことができるようになります。これはベトナムとの関係を深め、反中国同盟を強化することにもつながるでしょう。

Make no mistake: the future of Japan, with an American collapse, will be hard and difficult. But the Japanese people are hardworking and intelligent; I have faith in them.

　誤解のないように言っておきますが、アメリカの崩壊により日本の将来は厳しく困難なものになるでしょう。しかし、日本人は勤勉で聡明です。私は日本人を信頼しています。

Concerns about the new prime minister
新首相への不安

On September 27th, the Liberal Democratic Party held its presidential election, and after some confusion, Ishiba Shigeru was chosen. It seems that former Prime Minister Kishida backed him, although such information has not been made public.

　9月27日に自民党総裁選挙が行われ、混乱の末、石破茂氏が選出されました。公表されていませんが、岸田前首相も石破氏を応援していたという話が出ています。

As far as policy is concerned, after only a couple of weeks, it is difficult to predict what Prime Minister Ishida will do. He has mentioned deeper military cooperation with America. And he has spoken of creating an Asian NATO to counter China.

　政策に関して言えば、わずか数週間で石破首相が何をするかを予測するのは難しいです。首相はアメリカとの軍事協力の強化に言及しています。また、中国に対抗するためにアジア版NATOを創設

Chapter 3 What should Japan do?

するとも語っています。

Perhaps I should send him a copy of my book. I think to make intelligent policy for Japan's future, he should read it. In this book I have written much about American decline, which is well underway. Especially America's military. Rather than creating a strong fighting force, the American Left has created a weak and ineffective military that can actually accomplishes little.

　おそらく私は彼に本書を献本すべきでしょう。日本の将来について賢明な政策を立てるために、彼にはぜひ読んでもらいたいです。本書では、アメリカの衰退について多く書いており、それはかなり進行しています。特にアメリカ軍については紙幅を割いています。アメリカ左派は強力な戦闘力を作らず、実際にはほとんど何も達成できない弱くて無力な軍隊を作ってしまいました。

And the Ukraine war has shown American weaponry of all types to be outclassed by Russian weaponry of all types. America is a helpless giant. Does the new Prime Minister understand this? I don't think so. And this idea of an Asian NATO, as far as I can see, it is only four countries, the United States, Japan, South Korea, and the Philippines. No one else seems interested.

　そしてウクライナ戦争は、アメリカのあらゆる兵器がロシアに劣っていることを明らかにしました。アメリカは無力な巨人です。新首相はこのことを理解しているでしょうか？　私は理解していないと思います。そして石破首相が掲げた「アジア版ＮＡＴＯ」というアイデアは、私が見る限り、アメリカ、日本、韓国、フィリピン

の4カ国だけです。他の国は興味がないようです。

We have yet to see how the new Prime Minister will deal with the South Koreans, who are very difficult. They keep retreating into imagined historical wrongs. I don't think an alliance will work out well. This seems not to be a Japanese plan, but an American plan.

　新首相が、非常に扱いにくい韓国にどう対処するかはまだわかりません。彼らは想像上の歴史的過ちに逃げ込み続けています。同盟がうまくいくとは思えません。この「アジア版ＮＡＴＯ」は日本の計画ではなく、アメリカの計画のようです。

Americans do not study, that is why they come up with such unworkable plans, and then pressure other countries to adopt them. America right now is internally unstable, in fact, civil war is a distinct possibility.

　アメリカ人は勉強しません。だから、このような実行不可能な計画を思いつき、他の国々にそれを採用するよう圧力をかけます。アメリカは今、内部的に不安定で、実際、内戦が起こる可能性は十分に有ります。

Prime Minister Ishiba's tenure will probably be short, he will have no idea of how to deal with an America in crisis, or how to lead Japan without American guidance.

　石破首相の任期はおそらく短く、危機に瀕したアメリカにどう対

Chapter 3 What should Japan do?

処するか、アメリカの指導なしに日本をどう導くか、彼には何も分からないでしょう。

But I think it is evident that America wants an obedient Japanese Prime Minister. And they will interfere until they get it. However, as the American crisis gets worse, they will become unable to interfere in Japan's internal affairs. This time will come soon. We in Japan will have to survive until then.

　しかし、アメリカが従順な日本の首相を望んでいることは明らかだと思います。そして、それを手に入れるまで干渉するでしょう。しかし、アメリカの危機が悪化するにつれて、彼らは日本の内政に干渉できなくなります。その時はすぐに来ます。私たち日本人は、それまで生き延びなければなりません。

The nightmare of the 2028 Olympics
2028 ロスオリンピックの悪夢

The Paris Olympics has been extremely Left-wing. In 2016, the opening ceremony of the Swiss Saint Gotthard tunnel had very pagan features to it. But as far as I know, there were no transgenders involved. The Paris Olympic ceremony opening was quite different in this regard, openly Gay and transexual. Also, it deeply mocked Christianity.

　パリオリンピックは極めて左翼的でした。2016年のスイス・サンゴッタルドトンネルの開通式には、異教的な要素が色濃く反映されていました。しかし、私が知る限り、トランスジェンダーは関与

していませんでした。パリオリンピックの開会式は、この点ではまったく異なり、ゲイやトランスセクシュアルを公然と取り上げていました。また、キリスト教をひどく愚弄していました。

Also, the food and facilities were terrible. The food was vegan, in an athletic environment with young athletes that require large amounts of protein, which means meat. Also, the transport was a mess, and the cooling of the Olympic village buildings was non existent, all in the name of Leftist "SDGs" theories.

　また、食事と施設もひどいものでした。競技に出場する若い選手たちは大量のタンパク質、つまり肉を必要としますが、食事はビーガン料理でした。また、輸送は混乱し、オリンピック村の建物には冷房がまったくありませんでした。これらはすべて左翼による「SDGs」の名の下に行われたものです。

Well next the Olympics move to Los Angeles in California. And I am afraid that it will be even worse. Even if Donald Trump becomes President, California will still be a very Left-wing state.

　さて、次のオリンピックはアメリカのロサンゼルスに移ります。そして、状況はさらに悪くなるのではないかと心配しています。ドナルド・トランプ氏が大統領になったとしても、カリフォルニアは依然として非常に左翼的な州のままです。

Transgenderism is a cult religion there. California is also trying to achieve fewer emissions by having all cars operated by electricity. Yet there are few charging stations for electric vehicles; the States' electric grid cannot support it.

　トランスジェンダー主義は、カリフォルニアではカルト宗教です。カリフォルニア州はまた、すべての自動車を電気で動かすことで、排出量の削減を目指しています。しかし、電気自動車用の充電ステーションはほとんどなく、州の電力網はそれをサポートできません。

The opening ceremony is certain to be graphically transgender, the meals will be basically vegan, and there will be an emphasis on sustainability. And crime in Los Angeles is out of control. Can a Left-wing city government ensure the safety of visitors to the Olympics? I doubt it.

　開会式は間違いなくトランスジェンダーを全面に押し出し、食事は基本的にビーガン料理で、持続可能性に重点が置かれるでしょう。そしてロサンゼルスの犯罪は制御不能です。左翼の市政府がオリンピック訪問者の安全を確保できるでしょうか？　それは疑わしいです。

第 3 章　日本は何をすべきか？

Transgender boxer Imane Khelif sparks controversy at the Paris Olympics(2024)
パリ五輪（2024）で議論となったトランスジェンダー・ボクサーのイマネ・ケリフ

Afterword
おわりに

This book presents a very bleak view of the future of America. The 2024 election will be pivotal. Basically, a Harris victory means that America will continue on into the abyss of chaos, while a Trump victory will mean that a partial recovery could be possible.

この本は、アメリカの将来について非常に暗い見通しを示しています。そして、2024年の選挙は極めて重要なものとなります。基本的に、ハリス氏が勝利すれば、アメリカは無秩序の奈落の底へと落ち続けることになりますが、トランプ氏が勝利すれば、部分的な回復の可能性が出てきます。

Decades of chaotic Leftist policies and the three and a half years of the Biden administration, have left America in a very sad state. I have tried to chronicle these events in this book. And if Donald Trump becomes President, we must remember that many Americans will fight him and try to stop him from implementing any reforms. The possibility of him being assassinated while President will be high. And success is not guaranteed, merely possible.

数十年にわたる混乱した左派政策と、バイデン政権の3年半は、アメリカを非常に悲惨な状態に陥れました。私はこの本でこれらの出来事を記録しようとしました。そして、ドナルド・トランプ氏が大統領になった場合、多くのアメリカ人が彼と戦い、改革の実施を阻止しようとすることを忘れてはなりません。大統領在任中に暗殺

おわりに

される可能性は高いでしょう。そして成功は保証されておらず、単に可能性があるだけです。

And there will be much violence under a Trump Presidency. Under a Harris Presidency, there will also be much violence, as America disintegrates. Not much hope for anything there.

そしてトランプ大統領のもとでは多くの暴力が起こるでしょう。ハリス大統領のもとでもアメリカが崩壊するにつれ多くの暴力が起こるでしょう。そこにはほとんど希望がありません。

Yet there is another point to make. And this message is direct at the Japanese people. It is time to end our psychological dependence upon America. From now on, Japan will have to take a more independent course in international relations and economic policy.

しかし、私が言いたいことはもうひとつあります。これは日本国民に向けたものです。アメリカに対する心理的依存を終わらせる時が来ています。これからは、日本は国際関係と経済政策において、より自立した道を歩まなければなりません。

Remember, America is a failure in all respects, and the American-led world, the G7 countries, are all in a state of chaos. Leaders in Great Britain, France, and Germany continue to make bad decisions, and their societies continue to decline into Left-wing perversity and obscenity.

覚えておいてください、アメリカはあらゆる点で失敗しており、

Afterword

アメリカが率いる世界、G7諸国はすべて混乱状態にあります。イギリス、フランス、ドイツの指導者たちは誤った決断を下し続けており、それらの社会は左翼の異常性と低俗性を増して堕落し続けています。

Remember the awful French Olympics, the French are celebrating the death of their society.

ひどいフランスのオリンピックを思い出してください。フランス人は社会の死を祝っているのです。

Japan should not follow this. It is time to find our own way. Prime Minister Kishida exemplifies this. He worshipped foreigners. He kept pouring money into Ukraine, while Japanese who suffered from the Noto earthquake languished in despair.

日本はこれに倣うべきではありません。今こそ、日本独自の道を見つける時です。岸田首相はその一例です。彼は外国人を崇拝し、能登地震で被災した日本人が絶望に暮れる中、ウクライナに資金を注ぎ込み続けていました。

We must also think of the future. The future of the planet earth does not lie with America. At best, America will be struggling to survive. Rather the future of the Earth lies with Russia, and the BRICS nations, like India and Brazil. They have vibrant and healthy societies.

私たちは未来についても考えなければなりません。地球の未来は

おわりに

アメリカにかかっているわけではありません。アメリカは生き残るために苦闘するのに精一杯でしょう。むしろ地球の未来はロシア、そしてインドやブラジルのような BRICS 諸国にかかっています。これらの国々は活気に満ちた健全な社会を維持しています。

Recently, Russia is offering residence to people from Western countries who wish to live in a decent society. What a change from the old Soviet Union of 50 years ago, when I first came to Japan. And how America has declined.

最近、ロシアはまともな社会で暮らしたいと願う西側諸国の人々に居住地を提供しています。私が初めて日本に来た50年前の旧ソ連とは大きく変わりました。そしてアメリカは衰退しました。

Japan is going to have to revive its revolutionary spirit, similar to that the Meiji restration. This time, Japan will not need to adopt Western ways, but should look into its own soul, to rekindle the unique Japanese spirit. And apply that thinking to life in this modern world.

日本は、かつての明治維新のような革命精神を復活させなければなりません。今度は、西洋のやり方を取り入れるのではなく、自らの魂を見つめ直し、日本独自の精神を再び呼び起こすべきです。そして、その意識を現代の生活に活かすべきです。

It is time to leave the West behind to its fate, and reawaken Japan. I will help on this journey as much as possible. In this way, we will regain the respect of the nations of the world, and be revered as a truly innovative

Afterword

nation.

　今こそ西洋を捨て去り、日本を再び目覚めさせる時です。私はこの旅にできる限り協力します。こうして、私たちは世界の国々から尊敬を取り戻し、真に革新的な国家として尊敬されるようになるでしょう。

◆**著者**◆
マックス・フォン・シュラー（Max von Schuler）

元海兵隊・歴史研究家。ドイツ系アメリカ人。
1974年岩国基地に米軍海兵隊として来日、その後日本、韓国で活動。
退役後、国際基督教大学、警備会社を経て、役者として「釣りバカ日誌8」等、ナレーターとして「足立美術館音声ガイド」等、日本で活動。
YouTube公式チャンネル「軍事歴史がMAXわかる！」でも情報発信中。
著書に『［普及版］アメリカ人が語る アメリカが隠しておきたい日本の歴史』『［普及版］アメリカ人が語る 内戦で崩壊するアメリカ』（ともにハート出版）、『太平洋戦争 アメリカに嵌められた日本』（ワック）、『アメリカ白人の闇』（桜の花出版）、『アメリカはクーデターによって、社会主義国家になってしまった』（青林堂）などがある。

cover texture：Brusheezy.com

【写真提供】
P4左上：benkrut/PIXTA
P18：©David G. McIntyre/ZUMA Press Wire/共同通信イメージズ
P28：共同通信社
P31：©Joel Angel Juarez/ZUMA Press Wire/共同通信イメージズ
P114：共同通信社
P123：ロイター＝共同
P153：AP/アフロ
P201：新華社／共同通信イメージズ

アメリカ人が語る
沈む超大国・アメリカの未来

令和6年11月14日　第1刷発行

著　者　マックス・フォン・シュラー
発行者　日高裕明
発　行　株式会社ハート出版

〒171-0014 東京都豊島区池袋 3-9-23
TEL.03(3590)6077　FAX.03(3590)6078
ハート出版ホームページ　https://www.810.co.jp

©Max von Schuler 2024　Printed in Japan
定価はカバーに表示してあります。
ISBN978-4-8024-0183-8　C0021
乱丁・落丁本はお取り替えいたします。ただし古書店で購入したものはお取り替えできません。
本書を無断で複製（コピー、スキャン、デジタル化等）することは、著作権法上の例外を除き、禁じられています。また本書を代行業者等の第三者に依頼して複製する行為は、たとえ個人や家庭内での利用であっても、一切認められておりません。

印刷・中央精版印刷株式会社

世界に伝えたい！日米2カ国語併記
マックス・フォン・シュラーの本

[普及版] アメリカ人が語る
アメリカが隠しておきたい日本の歴史

一番読まれているマックス氏の本！

真実を語ること、それはヘイトスピーチではありません

元海兵隊員がアメリカの嘘を告発！「南京大虐殺」「性奴隷」「強制徴用」など反日の主戦場はアメリカ！ 米国は日本に永遠の贖罪意識をもたせることで日本を抑え続けている

新書判　本体1200円

アメリカ人が語る
内戦で崩壊するアメリカ

7年前の予言がズバリ的中！話題の書

元海兵隊が アメリカの崩壊を予見！ 不正選挙、嘘の裁判、無警察状態、不法移民――日本のメディアが書かない真実。

[普及版] アメリカ人が語る 日本人に隠しておけないアメリカの〝崩壊〟 すでにすでに分断を超え、一触即発――日米同盟に頼る日本は「対岸の火事」ではない！ アメリカの危機＝日本の危機！

新書判　本体1200円